TWENTIETH CENTURY PEOPLE

AMY JOHNSON

QUEEN OF THE AIR

TWENTIETH CENTURY PEOPLE

AMY JOHNSON

QUEEN OF THE AIR

BY GORDON SNELL

HODDER AND STOUGHTON
LONDON SYDNEY AUCKLAND TORONTO

British Library Cataloguing in Publication Data

Snell, Gordon
  Amy Johnson.
  1. Johnson, Amy – Juvenile literature
  2. Air pilots – England – Biography – Juvenile
  literature
  I. Title
  629.13′092′4   TL540.J58

  ISBN 0-340-25203-0

Printed in Great Britain for Hodder and Stoughton Children's
Books, a division of Hodder and Stoughton Ltd, Mill Road,
Dunton Green, Sevenoaks, Kent TN13 2YJ (Editorial
Office: 47 Bedford Square, London WC1B 3DP), by
Fakenham Press, Fakenham, Norfolk. Photoset by
Rowland Phototypesetting Ltd, Bury St Edmunds, Suffolk.

Contents

For

MAEVE,

with love and thanks.

Amy Arrives

It was May, 1930: nearly four o'clock on a Saturday afternoon. In Darwin, on the north coast of Australia, big crowds had gathered at the airfield a few miles out of the town. Many people had been there for hours, peering into the sky with their eyes screwed up against the glare, or scanning the horizon with binoculars. Planes roamed the air, their pilots also gazing into the distance, searching.

They were waiting for a 26-year-old English girl, Amy Johnson, the first woman ever to fly alone from Britain to Australia. Amy had had her pilot's licence for only a year, and had never before flown outside England – yet here she was, ending a successful 11,000-mile flight in a single-engined plane that had taken her halfway round the world in 20 days. She had come through monsoon rains and desert sandstorms, over jagged mountain ranges and across oceans teeming with sharks. Her courage and daring had already made her world-famous, with millions of people in many countries anxiously following her progress.

And now, the crowds at Darwin gave first a murmur, then a shout of joy, as fingers pointed, hats waved, and excited children were held up in the air to get a better view. There it was – the tiny plane with its double layer of wings, painted dark green, with its name, *Jason*, in silver lettering on the side. The girl in the cockpit, in goggles and flying-helmet, was shouting for joy herself.

When she set out, few people believed that she would ever complete the journey – yet here she was, landing in Australia! It was the first of many flights that earned the admiration of the world for Amy Johnson – Queen of the Air.

1
First Journeys

Even when she was a little girl, Amy Johnson liked setting out on long journeys on her own. Once, she decided to make a trip to 'The North', though she only had a vague idea what that meant. She took a coin from her money-box, and packed up the provisions she thought she'd need for a long, dangerous journey – some toffee and some sweets. She got on a bus and went as far as the terminus at the edge of the city. Then she started walking. After a while she felt tired, and decided to try and get a lift. The first car she waved at stopped, and the driver looked at her in amazement: he was a friend of her father's. He drove her straight back home, bringing to an end one of the earliest journeys of the girl whose solo flights would one day make her famous.

Home at that time was a red-brick terrace house in the fishing port of Hull, where Amy was born in 1903 – the same year that the Wright Brothers, in the United States, made the first-ever powered flight in an aeroplane. Amy's father, Will Johnson, worked in the family business, importing and exporting fish, but, like his daughter, he had a sense of adventure: when he was 21, he set out with three other men from Hull to join the Klondike Gold Rush in Canada. But he didn't get rich: he came back two years later, with just a few small nuggets of gold, which he had made into a brooch for the girl he married soon afterwards.

The Johnsons had three other daughters after Amy, although Mr Johnson very much wanted a son, and used to grumble: 'There are too many skirts around this house!' He was a fond father, but a stern one, specially strict about what the family could and could not do on a Sunday, which was a day of chapel-going, hymn-singing and Sunday School. As a child Amy didn't mind all this religion, particularly as her father used to pass her sweets during the sermon, and give her a penny if she knew the words of a hymn by heart.

Later on, the third daughter, Molly, was allowed to go home before the sermon – and her elder sisters, Amy and Irene, always wanted to be the one chosen to take her. Molly thought how nice it was to be so popular – until she realised that Amy and Irene simply wanted to miss the sermon themselves . . .

The two older girls, with little more than a year between their ages, used to play a lot together. One of their favourite games was trying to get right round the living-room without touching the floor, by jumping from one piece of furniture to another. Later, Amy wondered if this was an early sign of her liking for being up off the ground, as a pilot!

Amy loved reading, especially fairy-tales, in which she always pictured herself as the heroine. She often sat reading for hours, while her mother played the piano. Mrs Johnson was a skilled pianist, and besides playing classical works she accompanied family sing-songs with her daughters, the songs varying from madrigals to more jokey numbers like 'John Brown's baby has a cold upon his chest!'

Amy was the oldest of the four girls in the Johnson family. Next came Irene, then Molly. Betty was born later. Left: *their home in Hull.*

In those days there was no television or radio to provide home entertainment. Radio didn't arrive until the early 1920s, and the first sets were not exactly easy to listen to: for a long time the Johnsons had one that the family had to sit around in a circle, each with a pair of headphones on. Amy used to wish that her father would get one of the more modern sets, with a loudspeaker.

11

Before radio, there was at least the cinema to go to, and the Johnson family enjoyed their outings to 'the Pictures'. It was at the cinema that Amy saw her first aeroplane, in a newsreel. She was so thrilled by the sight of this machine taking off into the sky and then landing, that she sat through the whole programme twice, in order to see the plane again.

At home, when she wasn't reading, Amy spent some time developing photographs in a dark-room they had rigged up; and she liked to help her father by arranging and labelling his stamp albums. She was always a great letter-writer too, and wrote many long letters to her father when he was away on business trips. She hated housework and wasn't very keen on cooking, but she enjoyed sewing and knitting. All the girls learned to knit, and they even thought it was a rather bold and rebellious thing to do, for their mother had never learned – she had been brought up by a governess who told her that knitting was 'unladylike'!

*   *   *

Amy was 11 years old when the First World War broke out, in 1914. Hull was often bombed in night-raids by the German air-ships, the Zeppelins. When the air-raid warning sounded, the Johnson family used to shelter in the cellar under the stairs, though Mr Johnson would often take a look outside at the big machines rumbling across the sky. Amy liked to follow him out, but she was always chased back in again. She was never really frightened by the raids – in fact, she thought the strange aircraft looked rather graceful. Besides, it was exciting to have a break in normal routine, and be able to stay up late.

Apart from the raids, the War did not affect Amy's life very much. Soon after it started she went to a local secondary school called The Boulevard, where she led an energetic life: she played hockey, and enjoyed swimming, which she'd always been good at –when the family went to the beach, she used to worry her mother by swimming a long way out. She also liked flying through the air on the trapeze in the gymnasium, and she could play cricket as well as most of the boys: she was one of the few girls in the school who could bowl over-arm.

She was a bit lazy when it came to school work, until later when important exams came along – then, she wished she had worked harder, and did hours of homework every night to catch up. Considering her later achievements, it's odd that at school she found Geography was one of her weakest subjects. She was never good at getting to places on time, and school was no exception: one of the things she learned there was how to make up the most elaborate excuses for being late!

She was always a good leader, if sometimes a rebellious one. When she was told the school couldn't hold a swimming competition she wanted, Amy went ahead and hired the local swimming baths, and organised a competition herself. Another time, she decided to lead a rebellion against the hard, flat straw hats which were part of the school uniform. A lot of the pupils wanted to wear the softer, more stylish 'panama hats' instead, and a group of them agreed that they'd all come to school on a particular day wearing these instead of the hated straw ones.

At school, Amy preferred sports to books. She enjoyed hockey, swimming, cricket and gymnastics.

But when the day came, Amy was the only one who turned up in a panama hat – the others were all too scared to go through with it. After that, she didn't think much of the courage of schoolgirls!

Amy was keen on cycling, and the first bike she had was given to her by a relation. It had no brakes, but she got quite used to riding and controlling it – in fact, when she first rode a bike that did have brakes, the sudden stop when she used them pitched her off into the road.

She was only 12 when she first rode a motor-bike, and that ride was nearly a disaster. She got out her father's motor-bike, without permission, and set off down Park Avenue, where they lived. Everything was fine until she got to the end of the street, and realised she didn't know how to stop. She managed to do a U-turn and go back down the street again. By this time her parents were at the gate, shouting, and each time she wobbled past them she shouted back: 'How do you stop it?' But she could never hear the reply, and so she just went on going up and down the street, until the machine ran out of petrol.

After that, it was back to the ordinary bicycle, for the rest of her school career at least. Sometimes she played truant from school, and went for long bicycle-rides alone in the Yorkshire countryside. This liking for being alone was due partly to self-consciousness about her looks: she broke her front tooth when a cricket-ball hit her in the mouth, and it was some time before she could get proper dental treatment.

Amy took her exams, got a prize for French, and was offered a place at Sheffield University, where she thought she would study modern languages. The summer of 1922 was exciting and busy, as she prepared for University, bought new outfits and sewed name-tags on to everything. She celebrated her nineteenth birthday, and said she felt quite ancient!

*   *   *

There was another big excitement that summer, too: she began a flirtatious romance with a Swiss businessman called Hans, who had recently come to work in Hull. They went to the cinema together, and to dances, and occasionally for trips on his motor-bike – more safely than on that first escapade of Amy's . . .

The rest of the Johnson family were not exactly delighted with the relationship: for one thing, he was eight years older than Amy, and, though he was polite enough, he seemed stiff and reserved. Even young Molly didn't like him, although she was given small bribes by a boy up the road who fancied Amy, to let him know when 'the other one' had gone. Amy helped Hans with his English and, when she went to the University, they began writing long letters to each other. This romance grew into a passionate affair that went on for six years, and caused Amy a lot of unhappiness, though much later on she looked back and said that her father was quite right to oppose any marriage between Hans and herself.

But the friendship with Hans was only just beginning when Amy went to Sheffield, and it didn't prevent her from launching into the social life of the University – the parties, dances, and student debates. In some of her letters she teased Hans about her admirers; but she was less pleased when *he* wrote about the good time he was having. At Sheffield, Amy met Winifred Irving, another first-year student who became a great friend. They went for camping holidays together, and later on they shared flats in London.

Amy worried about money, and had problems managing on her allowance, though she was puzzled at where all the money went, even though one of her subjects was now Economics! She wrote home regularly, as well as sending her long letters to Hans, and every week she posted home a parcel of clothes which her mother used to wash and send back, enclosing surprise presents of chocolates, marzipan, or figs. Amy did, however, wash her own stockings, and darn them too, for many stockings then were made of silk, and if they tore, they were repaired rather than thrown away.

Amy had no very definite plans about what to do when she left University, though when she went there she thought of becoming a teacher. Then she had ideas of going into the Civil Service, or of getting a job abroad, in America, or perhaps in Switzerland . . . She was dreaming, too, of one day living in Switzerland permanently, as the wife of Hans.

But first there were the Final exams to get through. She studied hard, had a lot of headaches, and felt very tired. The six hours a day of the exams themselves were a strain not only for Amy, but for her student friends as well: one of them gave up halfway through, and another burst out crying suddenly during a church service. In one exam, Amy's mind went totally blank, and she had to close her eyes and sit still for ten minutes before she was able to go on.

To her great delight, she got through – but the degree-giving ceremony proved to be almost as nightmarish as the exams. Five minutes before-hand, she was told that everyone had to pay a fee of five pounds before they could take their degree. She rushed round her friends, borrowing a bit here and a bit there, and got the money together, with one minute to spare.

She was now Amy Johnson, B.A., and ready to go out into the world . . .

2

 # A Passion to Fly

Amy made a depressing start to her working career in the summer of 1925: she got a job in Hull, typing and answering the telephone in an accountant's office. She was paid one pound a week, and she hated it: so much so, that after three months she had a nervous breakdown and had to go away for a complete rest.

She stayed with family friends in Bournemouth, where Hans came to visit her. She was still hoping that she might be able to get a job in America, though she was worried about how that would affect her relationship with Hans.

When she was better again she got a job working in an advertising agency in Hull. She stayed there for a year, and in the summer of 1926 she went on holiday with Hans, for the first time. She thought of this Easter trip to Scotland as a kind of 'honeymoon', and was even more delighted when she persuaded him to take her to Switzerland a few months later. There she met his family and friends, but, in spite of their long romance, he still seemed much too vague when it came to the question of marriage.

When they got back she had rows with him, and rows at home too, though she was still able to go out and enjoy herself occasionally. One such trip was an outing with her sister Molly to one of the flying shows that toured the country at that time, giving 'joy-rides' to the public. Amy and Molly were taken up for a brief flight, for five shillings each. It was just a short circuit, without stunts: passengers who wanted to loop the loop had to pay extra, and the girls didn't have the money.

That was the first flight of the famous pilot, Amy Johnson, and she found it a bit disappointing – the noise, and the smell of petrol, made it all very different from the exhilarating experience she had hoped for.

It was two years before she flew again – and by that time, she had decided she wanted to learn to fly herself.

Meanwhile, she went to London and got a job in the silk department of a department store which had advertised for 'Ladies of Gentle Birth and Breeding'

While working in a solicitor's office, Amy lived in Maida Vale. Playing tennis at weekends, she noticed the planes of the London Aeroplane Club.

to be trained as sales-girls. The pay was three pounds a week, plus commission – but during training, the 'commission' was only what the store itself decided was the value of the work the girl had done. Amy got a note in her first pay-packet saying: 'Your services have been valued at four shillings and 7½ pence' – about 23p in today's money.

She left that job after four weeks, and got work in the office of a solicitor friend of her father's, where she stayed for three years. Much of that time, she shared rooms with Winifred Irving, her friend from college days. They lived in Maida Vale, not far down the road from the London Aeroplane Club's airfield at Edgware. There were tennis courts nearby, and when she was playing there Amy would sometimes stop in the middle of a game and gaze up at the Club's planes, circling overhead.

*   *   *

The London Aeroplane Club, formed in 1925, was one of the first of the flying clubs which the Government helped to set up, to encourage what they called 'air-mindedness' in the general public. There were already national airlines flying some regular passenger services: Britain's Imperial Airways had daily flights between Croydon and Paris, Zurich, Cologne and Amsterdam. But the flying times were slow, and bad weather often caused delays and cancellations – in fact, those who sneered at the unreliability of air travel used to say 'If you've got time to spare, go by air!'

Apart from the commercial transport planes, there were military fighters and bombers whose pilots were highly trained specialists, some of them the air 'aces' who did such spectacular and daring flights during the First World War. But there were very few privately-owned small planes, and not many people thought of flying as a sport for the ordinary man and woman.

The new flying clubs wanted to change all that, and they were helped by a new type of plane that first appeared on the scene in 1925 – the De Havilland Moth. The Moth was a single-engined plane with one propeller and two open-cockpit seats, one behind the other. It was a biplane, which meant that it had two layers of wings, one pair going straight across above the cockpits like a roof, and the other pair sticking out at the sides. The wings were joined to each other and to the body of the plane by a number of struts and wires. The Moth, like the flying clubs themselves, rapidly became popular with the public, who were encouraged to think of the plane as 'the motor-car of the air'. These Moths were the planes Amy stared at so eagerly, as they flew through the London sky.

One Saturday afternoon, she climbed on to a bus going north to Stag Lane, which led to the aerodrome. As the open-topped bus got nearer, the planes were so low as they flew towards the airfield that they almost seemed to be about to land on her head. Excitedly she got off the bus and ran up Stag Lane: there was a gate at the end, with a notice saying LONDON AEROPLANE CLUB. PRIVATE. There was no one about, so she went through the gate and walked on until she found herself on the edge of the airfield.

Two yellow planes were lined up, waiting to take

off. She saw a small clubhouse, with people sitting in deck-chairs in front of it – the kind of scene you might see at the edge of a cricket field. No one took any notice of her, so she went to an empty deck-chair and sat down. She looked round nervously, expecting at any moment that someone would come up and challenge her. But no one did, so she sat back and began to watch the planes.

For half an hour, Amy sat there enthralled. The planes were first of all started by someone standing in front of them swinging the propeller; then, when the engine roared into life, they taxied slowly across the grass, and finally gathered speed and rose up into the blue sky. The engines grew fainter, and the planes circling above seemed to make only a peaceful, purring sound as they ambled through the sky like free and lazy birds. Other planes, like birds that were more bustling and energetic, climbed and dived and swooped, and even looped the loop, making a perfect circle, their engines giving what sounded like a roar of triumph as the plane levelled out again.

Amy watched, fascinated: how she wished she could be up there, guiding one of those planes through the high air. She decided that, somehow, she just had to learn to fly. Looking around, she saw one of the flying instructors standing not far away, on his own, watching the planes. She summoned up her courage, got up and went across to him. She asked how much it would cost to learn to fly, and he told her the charges were two pounds an hour for instruction, and 30 shillings an hour to fly solo. The entrance fee was just over three pounds, and the annual subscription the same. And he said it took

Stag Lane Airfield, near Edgware, headquarters of the London Aeroplane Club until it moved to Hatfield in 1934.

between eight and twelve hours to learn.

Amy's heart beat faster – she could afford it! On the three pounds a week she was earning, it would mean saving and cutting down on other things – but it could be done. Realising she had a pound in her purse, she asked eagerly if she could start straight away. But the instructor said there was a waiting list of people wanting to join – her name would have to go before the Club's committee, and then she must wait her turn to be elected. But this didn't dampen her spirits: she made up her mind, there and then, that whatever sacrifices she had to make, she was going to become a pilot. She didn't then think of it as a career: she simply wanted to be up there in the sky, flying a plane all by herself.

As soon as she got home, she wrote to the secretary of the London Aeroplane Club, applying to be a member. The answer was disappointing – there was a long queue, and she would have to wait several months. She kept writing, and being told to wait; meanwhile she was able to join the Club as a non-flying member. But it was annoying to go there and watch others flying, without being able to have a go herself.

*   *   *

During that spring and summer of 1928, Amy's relationship with Hans came to an end. They agreed to be 'just friends', and even wrote to each other about new friendships. Amy certainly had plenty of admirers, but she still secretly hoped that she and Hans would get together again. She was very upset to learn, during the summer, that he had got married, without telling her he was going to.

At last, in September, she was made a full member of the Aeroplane Club, and thoughts of Hans could be pushed aside to some extent by the excitement of starting to learn to fly.

Her first lesson was not a success, and someone less determined than Amy might have given up the whole idea. In a borrowed flying-suit and helmet, she eagerly climbed into the cockpit behind the instructor, and the plane taxied out on to the airfield, and took off. There were two sets of controls, one in each cockpit, but because of the noise the instructor could only make the pupil hear by speaking into a tube connected to the earphones in the flying-helmet. The trouble was that Amy's borrowed helmet was much too big for her, and so the headphones in it, instead of being near her ears, were somewhere around her neck! All she could hear was a crackling burble she couldn't understand. Not realising what was wrong, she kept asking him to speak up – but it made no difference. They were in the air for 20 minutes, and Amy was nearly in tears with bewilderment and rage: this wasn't at all the exciting event she had been imagining.

The instructor wasn't sensitive to her feelings. He simply told her that she was absolutely hopeless – she would never learn to fly, and was only wasting her time and money trying.

Yet Amy wasn't going to give up. Not long afterwards, she had another lesson, this time with a kinder instructor, and a flying-helmet that fitted. She heard everything perfectly, and found the whole trip delightful – what's more, the instructor said he was pleased with her first attempt.

To pay for her flying lessons, Amy had to economise on clothes, meals and entertainment. Because of the cost, she couldn't have lessons as often as she would like, and the bad winter weather meant that sometimes, when she went to the aerodrome, no flying was possible. But the aerodrome and its new clubhouse became the centre of Amy's social life, where she could meet people as keen on flying as she was, pick up tips from them, and hear about the latest flying exploits.

By this time, flying as a sport was quite a craze – almost every weekend there were displays, air pageants, races, or flying-club meetings, all over the country. Crowds looked up and held their breath, as pilots did all kinds of aerobatics and stunts – there were even people who walked on the wings of aeroplanes while they were flying.

The big RAF displays at Hendon attracted over 100,000 spectators, but there were good audiences, too, at the smaller local shows put on by the flying clubs. Their little planes looped and swooped in the sky, flew upside down, and showed off their aero-batics – often known to the public as 'Crazy Flying'. There were some fairly crazy happenings on the ground, too: sometimes a spectator, in a city suit with a bowler hat and umbrella, would suddenly run out on to the field, jump into a plane, fly around in a dangerous-looking way, and make a heavy, bouncing landing. The audience were alarmed, until they realised that the 'spectator' was really a pilot from the club, and the whole thing was just an act.

In another kind of act, a 'runaway couple', driving across the airfield in an old car, would be bombed with bags of flour by the planes, and the car would be set on fire, while fireworks exploded. This was a small-scale imitation of the RAF display in which planes flour-bombed a wood-and-canvas fort manned by Boy Scouts dressed up in Arab robes – and this act, too, ended with a spectacular fire and fireworks.

Such events were certainly popular with the audiences, and helped to add to the funds of the flying clubs, though the clubs had a problem with what they called 'Hedge Guests' – people who came as far as the hedge surrounding the airfield, and watched the aerial displays for nothing.

But the thousands of enthusiastic club members were interested in more than providing circus-like entertainments. They felt themselves to be cam-paigners for a form of travel that could bring new excitement and hope to the world – a kind of inter-national fellowship of the air, uniting peoples of different lands in understanding and peace. This was certainly Amy's feeling: to her and people like her, Aviation was a gospel to be preached and spread. She saw it, with a simple kind of patriotism, as a force that would bind together the peoples of the British Empire, who made up about a quarter of the world's total population.

She and other flying enthusiasts would travel long distances to get a glimpse of the planes in one of the big air races – like the King's Cup Race, which was then a circuit of up to 1500 miles around Britain; or the Schneider Trophy Race, a contest for seaplanes – the planes with boat-shaped floats instead of wheels, which allowed them to use the water of lakes or the sea as a runway.

The aviation fans in the clubhouses could reel off from memory all the great achievements and 'Firsts' in the short history of flying. In the year 1919, there had been the first non-stop flight across the Atlantic by Alcock and Brown, from Newfoundland to Ireland; and in the same year, two Australian brothers, Ross and Keith Smith, made the first flight from Britain to Australia taking just under 28 days and winning an Australian Government prize of ten thousand pounds.

Both that flight and the transatlantic one were made in a bomber plane called the Vickers Vimy, but later came the pioneer solo flights in smaller planes. In 1927, Captain Charles Lindbergh flew his single-engine monoplane alone across the Atlantic from Long Island, New York, to Paris, in France. His average speed was just over 100 miles an hour, and the journey took him 33 hours and 39 minutes. The following year, 1928 – the year Amy

Amy Johnson

Johnson started flying – the Australian airman Bert Hinkler flew solo from England to Australia in 15½ days. That was the record Amy herself set out alone to try to break, only two years later.

Women pilots were still looked on as unusual, and many of them were people with titles, or money, or both, like Lady Heath, who had made a pioneer solo flight from South Africa to England and led a successful campaign against the ban on women becoming professional pilots. It was even more unusual to find a woman who knew anything about the engineering side of aircraft – yet Amy decided she wanted to learn how to maintain and overhaul aero-engines, as well as how to fly planes.

*   *   *

The moment Amy had been longing for since she started flying came in June 1929: her first solo flight. As she sat there at the controls, on her own, making the machine bank and turn and climb, she felt supremely happy: flying was now such a passion that she was ready to give up anything to indulge in it. That night she wrote home excitedly, saying that it wouldn't be long now before she'd done enough flying hours to get her Private Pilot's Licence – then she could take the family up for trips.

Less than a month later, she took the tests for her Licence, feeling as nervous as she had before her university exams. The tests included making accurate turns, approaches and landings, as well as answering questions about the rules of flying. Amy did well, and was soon proudly able to tell her family that she was a qualified, licensed Pilot.

Learning to fly.

She moved to lodge with a family that lived in North London, not too far from the aerodrome. She persuaded her father to lend her the money to buy their old car, when he decided to get a new one. She soon learned about the engine, and could tune it up, clean and maintain it – but it was proving more difficult to acquire the same sort of knowledge about aircraft engines . . .

Trying to improve that knowledge, she used to hang around on the fringe of the group of mechanics who waited to check the aircraft when they'd finished flying: but she found she wasn't at all welcome. The men felt uneasy with a woman there;

they didn't feel able to swear and joke in their usual way, and they certainly didn't believe a woman was capable of handling aircraft engines. Amy was determined to prove them wrong – but she might never have got the chance, if it hadn't been for the Club's Chief Engineer, Jack Humphreys.

He encouraged Amy's interest in engines, and even allowed her to come into the hangars and workshops, where he showed her how things were done. Amy started getting up at five or six o'clock in the morning, so as to spend some time at the aerodrome before going into central London to be at the office at 9.30. After work, she hurried back to the aerodrome, to do more flying, or to help in the workshops, or to sit chatting or writing letters in the clubhouse. She lived for the Club and the aerodrome, and the life and atmosphere she found there: work at the office became a drudgery that prevented her being where she really wanted to be.

The bold idea came into her mind: why couldn't she train to be a qualified engineer, and spend all her time among the planes she had grown to love so much?

3

Ready for Adventure

Amy's plan to work full-time at the aerodrome didn't appeal to her father – but eventually he agreed, and said he would give her a small weekly allowance for six months, and also the money to cover the cost of her training. Amy was delighted. Jack Humphreys prepared a busy study-and-work programme for her, and she got lodgings within walking distance of the airfield.

The weekend before she started work, she had a wonderful day out with friends from the Club, watching the planes in the Schneider Trophy Air Race, from a speed-boat in the Solent. But when she turned up at the hangars for her first day, eager to be one of the team, she found the other engineers and apprentices treating her either with amusement or with actual hostility: the Second Engineer had even threatened to resign if she was allowed in the workshops. She was given the worst jobs, like sweeping out the hangars. But she wasn't put off. She was absolutely determined to achieve her great ambition: to become the first woman ever to get a Ground Engineer's licence.

Amy's sheer guts, as well as her good humour, soon made the men accept her: she would tackle any job, however tough or dirty; she didn't worry if there was oil and grease all over her face, and her fingernails were chipped and broken. So it wasn't long before she was treated as 'one of the boys'. They even gave her a nickname, 'Johnnie', a shortening of her second name – and she was known affectionately as 'Johnnie' for many years, first by workmates and friends, and later by the people all over the world who followed her progress day by day as she flew to Australia.

Amy's routine, six days a week, with Mondays off, began when she started work at the hangars at 7.30 a.m.

She put on her stained overalls, and climbed the steps beside the plane whose engine she had been told to work on, carrying a grease gun, oil can, spanner and other tools. First she washed the engine down with paraffin, getting dirtier herself as the engine got cleaner! Then she began the detailed work of getting the engine into perfect condition for flying. She had to grease parts of the engine, clean the petrol and oil filters, test valve-springs and see the bolts on the propeller shaft were tight enough, as well as doing all kinds of other checks on the electrical system, pipes, screws and switches. If unscrewing a nut was very hard, she might shout for help to a man working on the next machine – and he might reply: 'Help yourself – to a bigger spanner!'

At the morning tea-break, they all trooped into the kitchen, and stood round a table, munching thick cheese rolls and drinking from huge mugs of tea. Then it was back to work, preparing the engines for the moment when the hangar doors rolled back and a procession of six yellow machines was wheeled out, with some men pushing at the front, and one man walking at the back, with the tail held on his

Amy worked on the planes from 7.30 in the morning till 6 in the evening, six days a week, before going on to lectures or studying for her engineering exam. She said she had never been happier in her life.

shoulder. Then the engines were warmed up ready for the flying instructors, while Amy and the other mechanics went back to the workshop to do overhaul and repair work on engines at the benches, or tackle such filthy jobs as scraping a cylinder-head that had got blackened with carbon.

Of course there was always the job Amy really disliked: sweeping out the hangar. The broom was bigger than *she* was, and the hangar seemed like some huge cavern, as she swept and swept the dusty concrete floor, thinking how much she had always hated housework . . .

Amy's working day went on till six o'clock, or sometimes later, and even after that she had to attend lectures, or study for her engineering exam. Yet she said she had never been happier in her life.

In November, only a couple of months after she had started work at the aerodrome, Amy was told the date of her examination – and it was only a few days ahead. There were no written papers, but a lot of practical questions from a board of five examiners. Amy faced them nervously, but she was relieved to find their questions easier than she had expected: in fact, so easy, that she began to wonder if they were trick questions, designed to catch her out. But she need not have worried. A few weeks later, the news came through that she had passed; the Air Ministry issued her with a Class 'C' Ground Engineer's Licence, the first they had ever given to a woman.

*   *   *

Amy was as pleased and proud of this success as she had been about getting her pilot's licence the previous summer – especially as Jack Humphreys had thought up a plan for her to fly a new plane that was being built by a young aircraft designer called James Martin.

James Martin later became famous as a designer, especially of the ejection seat which has saved the lives of so many pilots by catapulting them out of planes that are about to crash and bringing them safely down by parachute. His firm is now a big aircraft company, but at that time he had just begun, and his business was a very small one. He and Jack Humphreys thought that as a 'lady pilot' Amy would attract publicity both for herself and for the new Martin monoplane she would demonstrate.

Amy was excited about the plan because it meant that she would be doing a professional job as a pilot, and that was what she had always wanted since she took up flying seriously. The publicity would also help her to get further work in the future. She realised that there was a lot of prejudice against women in the professional aviation world, just as there was in so many other professions. She would have to prove that she was as good as the men – and indeed better than most of them – if she was going to get anywhere.

One of the instructors at the London Aeroplane Club once mentioned casually that flying to Australia would be a good way of proving what she could do. And eventually she hit on the idea that flying the new Martin plane to Australia would be the ideal way of showing off both the aircraft and her own skill as a pilot. It wasn't long before she found that her idea was making her headline news.

It happened almost by accident. Soon after she got

her Ground Engineer's Licence, a reporter from the *Evening News* was at the Stag Lane Aerodrome to interview another pilot, and someone mentioned that there was a girl working there as an engineer. It sounded like a good story, so the reporter asked to see her. Jack Humphreys thought it was a good idea, and Amy talked to the reporter. She said she hoped to make a long distance flight in a new plane which she could not yet reveal anything about.

Next day, there were headlines in the *Evening News*:

GIRL TO FLY ALONE TO AUSTRALIA
THE FIRST WOMAN AIR ENGINEER
AND HER PLANS
A SECRET PLANE

The reporter described how Amy stood talking to him dressed in thick shoes, woollen golf stockings, knee breeches and a leather tunic, swinging a flying-helmet in her hand, while the wind tore at her fair hair. He said she looked as if she should be a ballet dancer rather than a pilot. He got a lot wrong, saying she was 22 instead of 26, came from the Midlands instead of Yorkshire, and made a good living out of aviation. But the article certainly got the publicity Amy had been looking for: when she turned up at the aerodrome next morning, there were ten press photographers and a newsreel film-crew waiting for her, and her picture appeared in all the papers and on cinema screens all round the country.

Amy decided that now was her chance to use her new fame, to get financial backing for a flight to Australia.

The first woman air engineer.

There were a lot of expenses involved in such a journey. There was the fuel and oil, for a start; then there were spare parts, navigation aids, tropical clothes, and a large number of maps – these needed to be detailed maps, and they were quite expensive. And there was the money for ordinary living expenses too. Firms were sometimes willing to sponsor flyers to get publicity, just as today they might sponsor a sports event or an opera company. Newspapers would pay big money for the right kind of story, and some – particularly the *Daily Mail* – put up a lot of cash for competitions and for prizes for flying achievements. Sometimes, too, rich people who were keen on aviation, would give financial support to pilots.

But Amy found that getting people to back her turned out to be much harder than she expected. None of the firms she approached was interested. She looked through that directory of the famous,

37

Who's Who, and wrote to many of the titled people listed there, in the simple belief that people with aristocratic titles must also have money and be willing to spend it. Some replied courteously, turning down her request – others didn't reply at all.

It was the same with the newspapers: they were ready enough to make a story out of a girl pilot and her daring plans, but not so ready to pay out money to help her put those plans into practice. At one time, any paper in Fleet Street could have bought the story of Amy Johnson's flight in advance, for £25. None of them would: they all thought that if Amy got as far as Paris in one piece, she'd be lucky.

A lot of professional pilots felt the same way. After all, Amy had been flying for only a year and a half; she had made her first solo flight less than a year ago. She had, once, flown to Hull to see her family, and done some cross-country flying, but she had never even taken a plane across the English Channel. And this was the girl who planned to fly alone for more than 11,000 miles, all the way to Australia!

But Amy's parents, after first being very worried about the dangers, were soon convinced that she had the skill and the courage to make the flight. At her father's suggestion, Amy wrote asking for support from a new political party, the United Empire Party, suggesting that she could fly to other parts of the British Empire, as well as Australia, helping to bring the 'Mother Country' into closer contact.

At this time Britain was looked on as the centre of the Empire, especially by people in Dominions like Australia, New Zealand and Canada. Australians, for instance, who had never been to Britain would speak of it as 'Home', and think of themselves as British. Amy pointed out in her letter to the United Empire Party that the transatlantic flyer, Lind- bergh, had called his plane after his home-town in the USA, *The Spirit of St Louis*, and suggested she might call her plane *The Spirit of England*. But still there was no offer of help.

She made the same sort of appeal in a brief article she sent to the magazine *Flight*, which printed it in their page headed 'Airisms from the Four Winds', among other items about the Prince of Wales flying over the jungle in Kenya, and a sea- plane in Greece that had had a collision with a boat.

In the end it was the Director of Civil Aviation himself, Sir Sefton Brancker, who helped to get Amy the sort of backing she needed. She went to hear a lecture he gave to the Royal Aeronautical Society, in which he said he wished England would wake up to the possibilities of aviation. Amy wrote an en- thusiastic letter to him, saying that she hoped her own planned flight would help to create public confidence in air travel, and asking if he knew anyone who could back her. She wondered if he had seen her appeal in *Flight* magazine. The only trouble was that, in her eagerness, she forgot to sign the letter!

Luckily, Sir Sefton Brancker was impressed enough by what she wrote to track Amy down, through the magazine. He was equally impressed when he met her, and wrote to Lord Wakefield, the head of the big Castrol oil firm, recommending Amy, and Lord Wakefield agreed to give her some support.

At the same time, her parents decided that, if she couldn't get the money to buy a plane anywhere else,

Amy's parents helped her buy her plane.

Jason *was a Gipsy Moth. Amy had it painted green, and named it after her father's business.*

they would give it to her. There had been long delays in the making of the James Martin plane, so Amy decided to try to buy a Gipsy Moth, the kind she had been used to flying at the Aeroplane Club. At that time there were only just over 200 planes in private ownership in the country, but Amy was lucky to find one for sale which was already fitted with extra petrol tanks for long-distance flying. After only a few minutes trying it out in the air, she decided that this was the plane she wanted, and sent it for overhaul and respraying. She got it coloured green, with the name in silver lettering on the sides, near the front: the name *Jason*.

Besides being the name of the hero in classical literature, who went in search of the Golden Fleece, Jason was also the trade-name of Mr Johnson's firm, and many parcels of Jason Kippers were sent to the London Aeroplane Club, to the delight of Amy's friends and colleagues there. Now, the name Jason was about to become famous in a real-life epic adventure, and make Amy Johnson a heroine in the story of aviation.

4

 The Great Flight
Croydon to Baghdad

Amy set about buying all the things she would need for her journey across the world, and she spent a lot of time organising the trip. There were visas and travel permits to get, as well as the maps; and arrangements had to be checked to make sure that petrol and oil supplies would be ready at the various aerodromes on her route. She found out what she could about the likely weather she would meet on the way; if she left her departure too late, she would run into the rains and storms of the monsoon season in the tropics, and these could make it impossibly dangerous to fly. She decided that early in May would be the time to set off, and indeed it was Monday, May 5th, 1930, when her epic journey started.

Amy planned to begin her great flight from the aerodrome at Croydon, south of London, and she flew there the day before, from the Club's airfield at Edgware, escorted by four of the planes from the Club. Chief Engineer Jack Humphreys travelled with her, squeezed uncomfortably into the front cockpit with a tool-kit and one of the spare petrol tanks. Amy's father was at Croydon to meet them, and while Jack prepared to stay up all night doing the final preparations on *Jason*, Amy went to the Aerodrome Hotel and got to bed early, to be ready for the big day.

The Great Flight: Croydon to Baghdad

Her father woke her long before dawn, and she got up and had breakfast. By four o'clock in the morning she was at the hangar, greeting Winifred Irving, James Martin and other friends who had come to see her off. Representatives of Lord Wakefield's oil company, and of Shell, who had agreed to supply her petrol, were also at the aerodrome: so were some pressmen and photographers.

The darkness slowly gave way to daybreak. The weather report was not too good: there was fog over the English Channel. But Amy was determined to leave according to plan.

Her small plane looked heavy and lumbering as it was wheeled out of the hangar on to the tarmac. It was carrying much more than its normal load – for one thing, there were the two extra petrol tanks, helping to hold the total of 80 gallons of fuel: about four times what a normal Gipsy Moth would carry.

Croydon Airport, May 5th, 1930, early morning. Among the group who had come to wave Amy off were her father, Jack Humphreys, Winifred Irving, James Martin and representatives from the firms supplying her with oil and petrol. The spare propeller can be seen, strapped to the side of the plane.

Then there was the heavy spare propeller, tied on to the side of the aircraft with pieces of rope. And there were also all the other supplies packed into the locker and the front cockpit: tools and spare parts, tyres, a first-aid kit and medicines, a cooking-stove, an air-cushion, billy-cans, a sun-helmet, a mosquito-net, and even a revolver. (Amy said it reminded her of some strange village store!) She took a few spare clothes, too, but very few, although one newspaper said she had in her aeroplane 'A cupboard full of frocks'!

She did have a parachute with her, though she'd only had a half-hour lesson in how to use one, and had never made a jump. She took a sheath-knife, too, because she had been told that the Timor Sea, north of Australia, was full of sharks, and if she came down there she wanted to be able to defend herself against them.

Jason had only four basic instruments to guide Amy to Australia: an air-speed indicator, an altimeter showing the plane's height, an indicator for turning and banking, and one compass. Pilots of light aeroplanes like the Moth usually found their way by what is known as 'dead reckoning': steering the plane on a set course by the compass, for a certain length of time, worked out in advance. But the most useful aid to flying was simply looking down out of the cockpit at the ground below, and trying to spot recognisable landmarks. That was why railway lines and railway stations were so valuable for these early pilots: they could get down low enough to see the names on the station platforms! Roads and rivers were another useful thing to look for.

It was because of this reliance on what pilots could actually see that, when they had to fly at night, they tried to do so when the moon would be full enough to let them see the ground below.

Some of the bigger planes of this period did have radio, but very few of the small ones did. There was no radio in *Jason*, so Amy could get no instructions about her course, and people on the ground could only know where she was when they could actually see the plane. There was no way of signalling or giving an SOS if she was in trouble, and of course this was long before the coming of radar and the other navigational aids which pilots use today.

Yet Amy hoped to fly a distance of 800 or 900 miles a day, and reach Australia in 12 days – three days less than the record set two years earlier by Bert Hinkler. She even had the optimistic idea that she might turn round at Darwin and fly straight back again, to set up an England-Australia return-trip record, too.

The group of people waiting on the tarmac were huddled in overcoats to keep out the chill of the early morning.

Amy posed for photographs in her fur-collared suit, with her flying-helmet and goggles. There were goodbye wishes, and a farewell kiss from her father. Then she climbed into the cockpit. But as she settled herself into her seat, she sniffed and looked worried. There was a smell of petrol. There must be a leak somewhere. It was soon traced to one of the con-nections in a petrol-pipe, but repairing it would take a bit of time, so Amy went back to her room to get some more rest. It was still only half-past seven in the morning when she climbed into the cockpit again.

45

Amy posed for photographers before settling into the cockpit. Then she smelt petrol . . .

She began her take-off run, but as *Jason* gathered speed along the runway, she suddenly realised the heavily loaded plane was not going to get off the ground before reaching the boundary fence. She slowed and swerved to avoid a crash, and taxied back to start her run again. This time *Jason* just got off the ground before the boundary fence, and started climbing steadily into the sky.

The watchers on the ground smiled with relief, as they stood peering after the plane until it was only a faraway speck. But Amy was discovering another problem to add to the discomforts of her flight. Again, it had to do with petrol. She had to operate a hand-pump, with an action rather like a bicycle-pump, to get petrol up into the gravity tank in the upper wing, and it needed 40 strokes of the pump for every gallon of petrol. Whenever she pumped, the sickening smell of petrol fumes filled the cockpit – and she had to pump about 50 gallons like this, every day. There was nothing she could do about it, at this stage, except try to get used to the smell: the only alternative was to give up the flight, and she couldn't bear the thought of that.

It wasn't just the glory and the glamour of the flight that made her so determined: Amy was sure that flying had a great future as a regular, safe and reliable means of travel, which wasn't by any means everyone's opinion at that time. She wanted to play her part in building that future, by getting a good full-time job in aviation. But there were a great many pilots wanting jobs, and a lot of male prejudice against women: by demonstrating her skill as both pilot and engineer, this pioneering flight would show people that she was at least as good as any man.

So Amy knew she would never give up, whatever discomforts and dangers she had to face. The first of these, apart from the petrol fumes, was fog, which she ran into above the English Channel. She flew on, hoping for the best, and when it lifted she looked down to see land below. At first she was afraid she had flown round in a circle in the fog, and was back over England: but she soon realised she was across, and on her way towards Vienna, with over 700 miles still to cover.

*   *   *

She arrived at Vienna late in the afternoon, and got ready to check and overhaul the engine, just as she had promised her instructor, Jack Humphreys, that she would. But the Austrian mechanics laughed at the idea of a woman messing around with engines, and insisted on getting on with the job on their own. Furious, she decided there was nothing to do but leave them to it, and she went off in search of somewhere to sleep. There was no hotel nearby, but eventually an old caretaker gave her a bed in a room in the airport buildings.

On Tuesday, she was up at 4 a.m., and ready to go soon afterwards. But when she started the engine, she didn't like the way it sounded. She got out and had a look at it, discovering that the mechanics had not been as efficient as they boasted; the plugs needed cleaning. After rummaging in the packed front cockpit for the right tools, Amy did the job.

After that all was well, and she took off to fly another 800 miles east to her next destination: Istanbul, then known as Constantinople.

The petrol problem got worse: there was a new leak, and now, at every stroke of the pump, a jet of petrol spurted into Amy's face. It made her feel so sick, that she had to do all her pumping with her head out over the side of the cockpit to get clear of it.

There was still an hour of daylight left when Amy arrived at Constantinople on May 6th, and she would have liked to use the time overhauling her engine. But the Turkish officials took so long over the routine of Customs clearance that it was dark when she got back to the plane. She cleaned and checked the engine with the aid of the headlights of a car, and then got *Jason* filled up with petrol and oil.

The Turks were eager to help – perhaps a little too eager. When she asked if they could put the plane into a hangar for the night, some of them grabbed the tail and lifted it so vigorously that the nose pitched forward on to the ground. Luckily, Amy had put the propeller into a horizontal position a couple of minutes before, so no damage was done.

With *Jason* safely stowed in a hangar, Amy walked to a hotel in the village near the airport. There was still one problem that worried her, and that was whether she would be allowed to continue her flight at all.

She had gathered together almost all the documents and permits for her whole route – but the Turkish flying permit had still not come through by the time she left England. She did have letters of introduction from Sir Sefton Brancker, Britain's Director of Civil Aviation, and the local Shell representative took these and tried to track down one of the top Turkish officials who could sign a flying permit. He found that one of them was in his bath and wouldn't see him, and another was in prison; he finally located a third who was watching a show at a theatre, and got him to sign the permit during the interval.

There were more delays when Amy got to the airport at 4.30 in the morning, ready to leave. She was kept waiting two hours for the right people to examine her papers, and then she had oil-pressure problems with her engine, and had to sort those out with an oil change. There was still the petrol leak to be fixed, and she was helped with that by the mechanic of a visiting French plane. She got away finally at ten o'clock. The late start meant that she could not reach Baghdad that day, as she had planned, but would have to stop instead at Aleppo, in Syria.

On the way she had to cross a mountain range, the Taurus Mountains, their peaks hidden in a layer of cloud. She decided to climb above the clouds, but the engine started coughing and spluttering, and she had to come down below them again. With jagged mountains rising up on either side, she flew along a ravine, following the railway line she could see snaking through it at the bottom. She thought how, even if she crash-landed and survived in those wild mountains, she might still have to face the gangs of bandits that were said to roam there. Among the odder items she had in her baggage was a special message to bandits, asking them to guard her safely, and promising a ransom – but she doubted if fierce mountain bandits would take much notice of that, even if they could understand English!

*   *   *

The gorge below her twisted and turned, and once, as she rounded a corner, she ran straight into a bank of cloud, and could see nothing at all. She was travelling at over 100 miles an hour: it was like driving a car flat-out through a tunnel, with the windscreen completely covered in cotton wool. And she felt that somewhere, hidden in that cloud, the cruel mountains were pulling at the little plane, like a magnet.

She dived down to try and get below the cloud, and came out after half a minute to find herself hurtling straight towards a great wall of rock. She managed to turn the machine just in time, and flew on, feeling badly shaken. At last, she got through the mountain

50

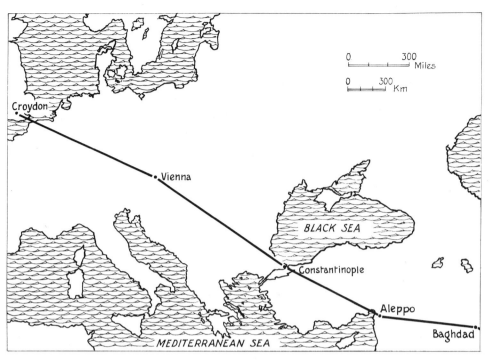

Croydon – Baghdad: Monday May 5th – Thursday May 8th.

range, and was flying over the vast plain on the other side, towards Aleppo.

The aerodrome there was run by the French Air Force, and their mechanics helped Amy do the daily overhaul of her engine. This was the first time she had been anywhere near a desert, and the hot emptiness of it, as well as the Arab robes and head-dresses of the local people, made her feel a sense of the mystery and romance of the East.

She left at dawn the next day, Thursday, May 8th, to fly 500 miles across that desert, to Baghdad. She nearly didn't make it. With most of the journey completed, Amy was flying at 7,000 feet towards Baghdad, when she suddenly ran into a desert sand-storm. She was blinded by the whirling sand, as the plane rocked and swayed in the battering wind, and

51

the struts and fuselage seemed to whine and groan. All at once, the propeller stopped turning, the engine gave out, and the plane dropped down like a stone, for at least 2,000 feet. Then it spluttered into life again, as the fog of sand swirled around and over it, blotting out any view and covering Amy's goggles.

Terrified, she struggled to control the machine – but then the engine stopped again, and again the plane fell down and down, with sickening speed. The engine picked up, only to stop once more, and *Jason* took another plunge downwards. Amy felt that she was being flung about by chaotic forces she could not control. Thankfully, she heard the engine come to life again, and realised that the clouds of sand were thinning out. She screwed up her eyes and peered through the sand only to get the greatest shock of all: she was only a few feet off the ground!

Desperately, she fought to get control of the plane, as it was blown this way and that by the raging wind. Once, she got a glimpse of Baghdad away in the distance – then the sand engulfed her again, and she could see nothing. The wind seemed to howl at her in mockery. She felt the wheels touch ground, though she still couldn't see anything. *Jason* bumped and swayed along, and Amy expected it would turn over or run into something, at any moment. But finally the plane came to a stop.

Amy switched off the engine and quickly jumped out. She caught hold of *Jason's* tail, which was bucking up and down like an untamed horse. She pulled the plane round so that it faced into the wind, which began to push it backwards. She clung on, and between the worst gusts of the wind, managed to get

Jason only had four basic instruments – and no radio. So the best way of navigating was simply to look down out of the cockpit and try to make out landmarks below. And that was difficult in bad weather.

some of her luggage out of the front cockpit, and wedge it under the wheels. She got out a canvas cover to try and keep the sand out of the engine, but in the fierce wind it took her half an hour to get the cover fastened on. Then she sat on the plane's tail, to keep it down, and waited for the storm to die out.

It was a long wait, while the sand blew around her, and got into her eyes, nose and mouth, and she thought gloomily that sand storms had been known to last as long as three weeks. Once, she heard dogs howling in the distance, and thought of the tales she had been told, of the savage wild dogs of the desert. Grimly, she took out her revolver, and waited for them to come looming out of the murk.

After three hours, the wind began to blow less furiously, and visibility became clearer. Seizing the chance, Amy uncovered the engine, and ran round collecting up her luggage. Fortunately, it took only one swing of the propeller to start the engine, and soon Amy was airborne again, flying in the direction where she thought Baghdad ought to be . . .

5

The Great Flight
Baghdad to Singapore

Amy got to Baghdad without further trouble, but when she landed there, one of the undercarriage struts broke in two, and *Jason* swung round, sinking on to one wing. The strut must have been weakened by Amy's 'blind' landing in the desert, at more than 100 miles an hour. This aerodrome was staffed by British employees of Imperial Airways, and Amy left the overhauling of *Jason* to them. However, they had no strut to replace the broken one; in the end, the old strut was sent across to the Royal Air Force base nearby, and mechanics there worked all through the night making a complete new one.

Amy was able to relax for a few hours, and she was taken on a sight-seeing tour of the city. When she got to the aerodrome next morning, on the Friday, *Jason* was ready to go, with the new strut in position. Amy climbed into the cockpit, wearing a pair of borrowed shorts, recommended to her as the most comfortable clothes for this kind of climate. And indeed, the heat was tremendous, as she flew along the mountainous shore of the Persian Gulf, looking down at the vivid blue water. She was worried about oil pressure, and the spluttering sound her engine began to make, but she finally reached her destination: the fishing port of Bandar Abbas at the mouth of the Gulf.

The Great Flight: Baghdad to Singapore

She landed heavily, on the large unmarked open space that served as an airfield. As the plane came to a halt, she was horrified to see the left wing drop, and trail on the ground. The bolt fastening the top of the new strut had broken. When she climbed out, she was met by the British Consul, whose house was just beside the airfield. She had a blinding headache, and felt too ill to do anything about her machine, but the Consul told her he had an excellent mechanic, who looked after his car and would do everything he could for Amy's plane. Amy felt too bad to argue, so she allowed the Consul's wife and daughter to give her tea, and show her to a bed where she could lie down. By dinner-time her headache had gone.

It was 10.30 p.m. by the time dinner was finished,

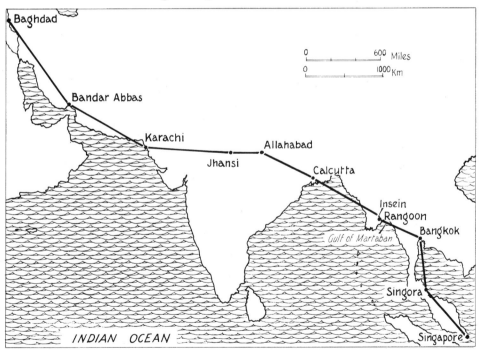

Baghdad – Singapore: Friday May 9th – Sunday May 18th.

and there was still the overhauling and checking of the engine to be done. When Amy got to the plane, she was amazed to find it standing up properly, with the wing fixed and a new bolt fitted. She was introduced to the Consul's mechanic, David, who said he had picked up some knowledge of aircraft engines when Air Force planes had been using the aerodrome, and he had found the bolt in an old box of spare parts.

With David's help, Amy carried out her regular overhaul of *Jason*, working by the light of the big moon that had risen, and using a torch for the fiddly 'inside' jobs. By the time they had finished, it was after two o'clock in the morning.

Yet Amy was up again at four o'clock, preparing for the 700 mile flight to Karachi in India. (It is now in Pakistan.) It took her nine hours; again the heat was tremendous, and again she was worried by a spluttering sound in the engine. She couldn't think what could be causing it, as she had put right the faulty plug that was at the root of the trouble the day before. Later on, she found that David had adjusted one of the plugs wrongly, and it had got so near the metal engine-cover that sparks had been flashing across the gap, all through the trip. If the plug had been one near the carburettor, the sparks could have made the whole engine catch fire – but Amy was lucky, and *Jason* landed safely at Karachi, on Saturday, May 10th, one of the hottest days on record, with the temperature reaching 110 degrees Fahrenheit in the shade.

It was the sixth day of her flight: she had now travelled more than 4,000 miles, and broken the speed record for a flight from England to India by a whole two days! The previous record had been held by Bert Hinkler, the same pilot whose England-to-Australia record Amy was even now trying to beat.

*   *   *

When news of the record to India was known, Amy became an instant celebrity, and her flight was headline news all over the world. She was called 'The Girl Lindbergh', after the lone transatlantic flyer, and since he had been nicknamed 'The Lone Eagle', she became known as 'The Lone Dove'. Hull was wild with excitement, and the whole Johnson family found that they were instant celebrities, too. Reporters called at the house, and Mr Johnson talked about his enthusiasm for Amy's flight, while her two youngest sisters told how she had bought a revolver before she went, and practised shooting at a row of medicine bottles. (Sadly, there were now only two sisters, Molly and the youngest child, Betty, to glory in Amy's success: Irene had died tragically the year before, by taking her own life.)

Mr Johnson and Jack Humphreys were pursued by the editors of those same newspapers that had turned down the story of the flight before Amy left. Now they were prepared to pay big money for it, and before Amy reached Australia Mr Johnson had done a deal on her behalf with the *Daily Mail*, which began to publish her own exclusive story of the journey. But neither Amy nor her father realised yet just how big the story was going to be . . .

At Karachi, Amy was pleased to get a cable from her parents: 'BEST LUCK. KEEP IT UP. YOU ARE

DOING SPLENDIDLY. THERE IS GREAT IN-
TEREST HERE IN YOUR FLIGHT.' And she sent a
brief cable back: 'ARRIVED SAFELY. THANKS
FOR WIRE. AMY.' She stayed as a guest in Government House and was given a reception.

Karachi was another of the Imperial Airways
aerodromes, like Baghdad, and their officials told
her to be a wise girl, and rest for a day while they
overhauled her plane. But she was determined to
press on, and after a lot of persuading, they agreed
to work on it overnight.

Next morning, as Amy prepared to leave, there
was a farewell ceremony at the aerodrome, and she
had garlands put round her neck and was presented
with a bouquet. An RAF plane and one from the De
Havilland Company escorted *Jason* for the first part
of the journey towards her next stop, Allahabad.

Strong headwinds upset her calculations, and
when she landed at what she thought was Allahabad,
she was still 200 miles away, at a place called
Jhansi. When she realised this, she took off again
at once, but after an hour's flying, her petrol was
getting low, and the daylight was starting to fade,
so she was forced to turn back to Jhansi again.

She landed there on the largest space she could
find, which turned out to be a military parade-
ground. *Jason* ran across it, and collided with a post
on the far side, damaging the front edge of one wing.
A carpenter from the nearby village was able to do
an excellent repair job on it, while the tailor patched
and sewed the wing.

Amy was helped with her engine overhaul by
officers of the regiment whose parade-ground she
had landed on. After a while they saw she was very

tired, and brought out a camp-bed which they put beside the plane. She was able to relax on this and direct operations, while servants came to and fro from the barracks with long, cool drinks. She said it was the nicest possible way to overhaul an engine!

She was able to get enough petrol at Jhansi to fly on early the next morning to Allahabad, where she was reported as saying, as she jumped out of the plane: '40 gallons, please! I'm in a hurry to go on!' And on she went, for another 460 miles, flying into strong headwinds and reaching Calcutta at six o'clock in the evening of Monday, May 12th.

She looked tired, and her face was sunburned and starting to peel, but she told reporters that she felt very fit, although she had been having only three hours sleep a night, and living mostly on a diet of

At Calcutta, Amy told reporters her main problem was finding clean clothes: those she had often became soaked with petrol. She slept three hours a night and lived mainly on sandwiches and fruit, which she ate while flying.

sandwiches and fruit, which she ate while she was flying.

What she did want was some clean clothes to borrow – and everywhere she stopped people were happy to give her shirts and shorts, and even dresses. It was just as well, because clean clothes became quite a problem: when the front petrol tank was filled, it often overflowed, and the petrol ran into the cockpit where some of Amy's clothes were stored. The result was that she sometimes had to go to bed in petrol-soaked pyjamas, laying out the rest of her things to dry overnight.

But clothes were a minor problem indeed, compared with what Amy had to face after she left Calcutta on Tuesday morning to fly the 650 miles to Rangoon in Burma. There was monsoon weather all along the route, with high winds and driving rain – it was the worst weather she had ever experienced, and she struggled for hours to get *Jason* through it. She could hardly see anything and, after crossing the coast of Burma, she was flying low to try to get a better view.

Suddenly, she saw a 12,000-foot-high range of mountains straight ahead. She managed to turn the plane away from them, and then fly around, gaining the height she needed to get across. After that, with visibility again appalling, she came down low once more, and started to follow the railway line towards Rangoon. The airfield at Rangoon was also used as a race-course, and when she thought she saw it, Amy came thankfully in to land.

Unfortunately her landing place was actually the playing-fields of an Engineering Institute at the jungle town of Insein, ten miles north of Rangoon.

Jason ran smoothly past the goal-posts, crashed into a wire fence, and ended up nose-down in a three-foot ditch, with the propeller broken, one of the wings smashed, a tyre ripped open, and the undercarriage damaged.

It looked like the end of *Jason*'s journey, and Amy was in tears as she climbed out of the plane. The principal of the Institute and his wife, Mr and Mrs Shaw, brought Amy into their house and gave her some clean clothes; she had a bath and a meal, and then they went, carrying huge umbrellas, out into the rainy night, to look at *Jason*. They had to cross the field which was like a sea of mud: mud which probably saved the plane from an even worse crash, by slowing it down a bit.

Though it was night-time, it was very hot, and the air was alive with insects. By the light of lamps and torches, a big crowd of local people and students from the Institute lifted *Jason* across the ditch and wheeled the plane to a more sheltered spot under some trees. Amy was in despair as she saw just how much damage there was – but Mr Shaw said cautiously that he couldn't promise anything, but he thought something could be done . . .

Next morning, he got everyone at the Institute working to help Amy, and a lot of people from the surrounding district too. The spare propeller was untied from the side of the plane, and put on instead of the broken one. The students straightened out the bent metal, and made new bolts, struts and fittings. A local rubber company representative got the tyre repaired. A Forestry Inspector gathered up the broken ribs of the wing, and glued them together like a jigsaw puzzle, to see exactly what their shape

61

and size was. Then he got some timber and made exact copies. But there was no aeroplane fabric to cover the wing, and none of the special glue called 'Dope', used to stretch and harden the fabric. A chemist from Rangoon was able to mix a glue very like the real thing, after merely sniffing the smell from an empty tin of it.

The fabric was more of a problem – until someone remembered that over ten years ago, after the First World War, there had been a big batch of spare aeroplane fabric sold off cheaply in Rangoon, and much of it had been made into shirts. A search was made in the cupboards, and several piles of these shirts were found and brought out. They were torn into strips, and sewn together by local sewing-girls.

As well as all this, the engine had to be over-hauled and cleaned again, after the coating of mud had got on to it in the ditch, and the new wing had to be fitted.

People worked in relays, carrying on all that day, through the night, and on into the next day. The heat was stifling, even during the night; the rain poured down in torrents the whole time, and the flying insects were around in such hordes that the people working had to have others standing beside them whose only job was to wave the insects away.

By late afternoon on the second day, Thursday, all the repairs were finished, and it was decided to tow *Jason* the twelve miles to Rangoon race-course, ready for take-off the next day. The local fire-engine was brought, and *Jason*'s tail was tied to the back of it. A policeman with a huge umbrella went ahead on a bicycle to clear the road, as the strange procession moved along at walking pace, stopping every 15

There was monsoon weather all the 650 miles from Calcutta to Rangoon. Amy landed on what she thought was an airfield, but it was the football ground of the Engineering Institute at Insein. Jason crashed into a fence and broke a wing and the propeller. It might have been the end of the journey, but the engineering students decided to help. Then, in pouring rain, the plane's tail was hitched to the local fire engine, and Jason was towed 12 miles to Rangoon. There, Amy set off again from the race-course which served as an airfield.

minutes to give the tyres a chance to cool down. The rain went on pouring down as darkness fell, and the procession continued its stately progress, lit by flaming torches that fizzed and spluttered in the wet. It took three hours to reach the race-course.

Amy was back there early the next morning, on May 16th, looking full of health and energy, wearing her socks rolled down over her shoes, as usual, and khaki shorts, a white sweater, and a raincoat. She certainly needed the raincoat, because every ten minutes there were downpours of drenching monsoon rain, followed by bright sunshine.

It was raining so heavily when she finally took off, that when she turned to wave farewell to the people at the airfield she couldn't even see them. Visibility was still bad as she crossed the Gulf of Martaban, much feared by pilots because of its treacherous weather. Once across that, she approached the mountain range that lay across the path to her next destination, Bangkok.

She knew there was a pass through the mountains at a place called Moulmein, but after half an hour flying around and peering through the cloud and rain, she still couldn't locate it. She decided to fly up to 10,000 feet and then try to get across. There was a lot of cloud at that height, and whenever it cleared a little, she started to descend – but each time there were still mountains down below. At last she did get down through a gap in the clouds, and was delighted to see a river. Flying lower, she realised it was the river that flowed down to the sea near Moulmein: she was still on the wrong side of the mountain range!

She climbed once more to 10,000 feet, through the

soaking clouds, and flew blind in what she hoped was the right direction; and she was eventually rewarded by the sight of the plains on the far side of the range. It had taken her three hours to get across those mountains – a journey that should normally have taken only half an hour.

Amy reached Bangkok aerodrome at 6.30 p.m., and was welcomed by a crowd of about 1,000 Siamese. After nine hours flying in those appalling conditions, she had a terrible headache, and went to get a little rest, while the airport mechanics began to overhaul her plane. She joined them later on, and it was a long job: for one thing, there were language problems, particularly with technical words, and for another, there was no lighting in the hangar, and they had to work by the light of Amy's small torch.

Jason was in the air again soon after dawn the next morning, with good weather for a couple of hundred miles; but then the storms came on again. This was the worst weather yet, and it lasted for 250 miles of flying. The only thing Amy could do was to keep very low, sometimes down to 50 feet, so that she could see the coastline, and follow it southwards. The rain was like a solid sheet of water, and she could see nothing through her flying goggles – so she took them off, and flew with her head out over the side of the cockpit, her stinging eyes feeling as if they were being torn out of her head.

*   *   *

For five hours she flew like that, following every twist and turn of the coastline. Once, she went

65

astray and discovered she wasn't over the coast at all, but was flying round and round above some flooded fields. Finally she got through the rain, and after flying another 50 miles she landed at Singora just before three in the afternoon of Saturday, May 17th. She realised it was too late to go on to Singapore that day, so she immediately began over-hauling the aircraft.

The airfield at Singora had no hangars, and was little more than a stretch of tarmac beside a sandy seashore: sand blew about constantly as Amy worked, and the tools got scorching hot in the sun.

The police roped off the area around *Jason*, which was just as well, because the local people regarded Amy and her plane as great entertainment, and there was soon a crowd of people sitting around with picnics, chattering and pointing and laughing happily. When Amy needed help with a particularly tight nut or screw, a strong man was found in the crowd to help her. Whenever she needed him she called out: 'Where is the strong man?' and the crowd got to know the words. After that, when she looked round for help, they all shouted: 'Strong man! Strong man!' and hooted with laughter. It was such a merry scene that Amy couldn't help laughing herself, which delighted the crowd even more.

The people came back in even greater numbers next morning to watch Amy take off. There seemed to be thousands of them: chattering men and women, Buddhist priests in long bright yellow robes, and hordes of children laughing and playing. They were standing in rows six or eight deep, on each side of the runway, almost like human hedges. Police were trying to keep the crowds back, but the children in the front kept edging forward, determined not to miss the fun. Not far from the end of the runway were some houses and a row of tall trees. It was going to be a difficult take-off . . .

After a lot of arguing and coaxing, the people were persuaded to move back a little, but there was still only a narrow path for *Jason* to move along. Any slight swerve to right or left would send the plane plunging into the crowd. Fearful of what could happen, Amy climbed into the cockpit. As *Jason* moved forward, she leaned out of the left side of the plane and looked ahead at the runway lined with excited, smiling faces. The plane gathered speed, and just as it rose from the ground, a spray of petrol from a vent-pipe spurted straight into Amy's eyes, and for a moment she could see nothing at all. She took the plane upwards, hoping desperately that it was still on a straight course. Then, to her great relief, she saw the line of trees below her, and the crowd in the distance, waving and cheering happily. She kept turning and waving back, until they were out of sight. Then she put *Jason* on course for the 470-mile flight to Singapore.

6

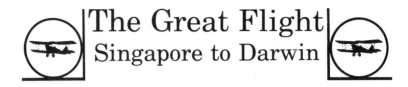

The Great Flight
Singapore to Darwin

That Sunday, May 18th, the weather, for once, was good to Amy, and in spite of a head-wind she made good time on the journey.

She landed at Singapore just before two o'clock in the afternoon, and the crowds that greeted her at the aerodrome were quite a contrast to those who had seen her off at Singora that morning.

Many of them were European women, wearing elegant dresses of muslin, lace and chiffon in bright colours, and they waved parasols and flimsy handkerchieves as she landed. Amy's oil-stained face smiled back at them.

She was wearing khaki shorts, the coat of a man's tropical drill suit, with a purple blouse underneath it, and one of those hard tropical sun-helmets called 'solar topees'. Her face was burnt almost brick-red by the tropical sun. The group of women all clapped their hands, and one onlooker said it was such a polite and dignified welcome, you'd have thought Miss Johnson had just finished singing a song at a charity concert, rather than flying solo all the way from England in 14 days.

But meanwhile, back home, Amy was being hailed as a heroine. Congratulations came from the Prime Minister, the Director of Civil Aviation, pilots like Bert Hinkler, and hundreds of ordinary people.

One London theatre even told Amy's father that they would like to put her into a stage show. It didn't matter now that delays and accidents had made it impossible for Amy to beat Hinkler's record: her cheerful courage had made her the idol of people all over the world, and in Australia, they were preparing a welcome such as had never been seen before . . .

Jason took off from Singapore at ten past six the following morning, heading for Sourabaya, in Java. Amy planned to follow a route along a chain of islands, but soon after leaving Singapore the plane was engulfed by a violent rainstorm, and she could see nothing at all. She brought the plane down lower and lower, to try and find the coastline and get her bearings – sometimes she was almost skimming the

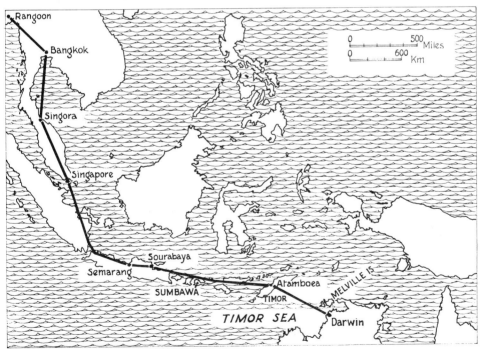

Singapore – Darwin: Monday May 19th – Saturday May 24th.

crests of the waves, with her altimeter registering the plane's height as Zero. It took her three hours to get through the storm, and to make up for lost time she decided to head out across the open sea, a more direct route than following the islands.

She finally crossed the coast of Java at 4.30 p.m., over ten hours after leaving Singapore. Darkness would be falling before long – and in that part of the world, near the Equator, there is no twilight.

There wasn't time now to reach Sourabaya, so Amy headed for a nearer town called Semarang. Then she discovered that she was nearly running out of petrol – she made a forced landing on the most likely open space she could see, which turned out to be the grounds of a sugar factory at Tjomal. Unfortunately there were some bamboo stakes sticking out of the ground in the path of the plane, and their sharp ends ripped into the wings. When Amy clambered out, she found that there were five holes, each about eight inches across, in the wing fabric.

The manager and employees of the sugar factory, who had gathered round, wondered how they could help. Then someone suggested sticking plaster. The First Aid cupboard was raided, and *Jason* really began to look as if he'd been in the wars, as strips of plaster were stuck on his wings to patch them up.

The next problem was fuel. The factory had no aeroplane fuel, but they did have some motor spirit. Amy took it gratefully, and carefully poured it into the tank, through two layers of chamois leather, to act as a filter. Even a drop of water or a grain of dirt could choke the fuel jet in the engine, and there were many stories of forced landings caused like that.

Amy stayed that Monday night at the manager's

house, and next morning she faced the problem of taking off again in the restricted space, without spearing *Jason*'s wings a second time on the sharp bamboo. Fortunately there was a slightly larger field not far away, and *Jason* was pushed along to that. Amy took off successfully at 8.45 a.m., and flew to Semarang, where she landed to refuel.

She was surprised and touched by the warm welcome she got, from both aerodrome officials and the public, but what pleased her most was the generous praise of the pilots stationed there.

They told her that there were two airports at Sourabaya, where she was heading, and the right one was difficult to find – so they suggested that she should follow a Dutch air mail plane which was about to fly there. The pilot of the three-engined plane said he would go as slowly as possible so that she could keep up. But when they were airborne, she found it very hard to match his speed.

They were flying above the clouds, and Amy knew that down below there were mountains and volcanoes, so she was determined not to lose her guide – even though it meant that she had to fly at 100 miles an hour, the whole way. When she landed at Sourabaya, the engine began to splutter, and the propeller stopped dead. *Jason* came to a stop, like a runner who flops down exhausted after an all-out race.

The propeller they'd put on at Insein was looking very much the worse for wear after battling through the heavy monsoon rains, and Amy was worried whether it could stand up to any more strain. Someone contacted a local man with a Moth plane. He promptly sent his own propeller to be fixed to *Jason*.

71

The airport mechanic who was overhauling Amy's plane worked all night on it, and she arrived before dawn to test the engine. It was still spluttering. Repairs and replacements were made, but it all took so long that there was no chance of doing any flying that day. At least Amy was able to catch up on her sleep, wash her hair, and get her clothes washed.

At dawn the next morning, Thursday, May 22nd, she took off to fly the 750 miles to Atamboea, on Timor Island. The sun was shining and the world looked beautiful, and Amy flew along, singing from sheer joy. At half past eleven in the morning, she was seen flying over Sumbawa Island, nearly halfway to her destination. At Atamboea they waited to greet her. They peered at the sky until darkness fell, but there was no sign of *Jason*, and no news of her coming down anywhere else.

For nearly 24 hours Amy's family and friends, the newspapers, and people all over the world waited for news. There were fears that she had plunged into the sea she always dreaded – the Timor Sea, with its sharks.

In fact she was safe – but only just. She had flown on towards Timor Island, and reached the final stretch of over 100 miles across open sea. Darkness was approaching when she finally spotted the coast, but she still had to find Atamboea. Below her there were mountains, 9,000 feet high; she climbed high above them, peering down and trying to see an airfield – but there was no sign of one. There didn't seem to be any flat piece of ground at all, where she could land. She flew round in circles, feeling very lonely indeed, and wondering if this was to be the end of her journey, with *Jason* crashing down

Jason *battles through stormy weather.*

into those jagged mountains, never to be found.

At last she saw a clearing, and brought *Jason* down bumpily, on rough ground scattered with stunted bushes and ant-hills.

She sighed with relief as she climbed out of the plane, but the relief turned to fright, as she heard shouts, and saw dozens of men rushing towards her, waving spears and knives. They surrounded the aeroplane, talking excitedly, and Amy wondered what they were going to do. Then a big man, who seemed to be a leader, smiled at her and made a gesture of salute. He began talking to her, but there was only one word she could understand: the word, 'Pastor'. She realised there must be some kind of Church Mission nearby. The leading tribesman took her hand, and led her after him, through the darkness, with the others following.

They walked for miles over the hills, and came to a small church. Exhausted, Amy sat down against the wall of the porch, and in spite of the chattering going on all around her, she fell asleep. She woke suddenly when someone tugged at her arm: there in front of her was a dignified old man with a long beard, bowing low. The sight was so odd that she laughed nervously; the Pastor smiled, and the group of tribesmen gave a cheer. She shared a meal with the old man, and he was just showing her to a room when they heard the sound of a motor-horn.

It was a group of officials from the aerodrome at Atamboea; they had heard the sound of her plane, and come out to search for her. The place where she had been brought was called Haliloeli, and it was only 12 miles from Atamboea. But there had been a bush-fire at the airport recently, and the ground was burnt black, so that it looked from the air like a patch of dark scrubland. Amy realised she must have seen it, without knowing what it was.

She went back with the airport people to stay in Atamboea's only hotel, a ramshackle place with the hardest bed Amy had ever known.

The next morning she was taken back to *Jason*.

The Pastor had some drums of motor spirit in a shed near his church, and they had to be brought over the hills by donkey to where *Jason* was. When they arrived, Amy tried for an hour to get the petrol to go through her chamois leather filters into the tank, but without success.

Amy decided she would just have to hope that the small amount of petrol left in the tank would get her as far as Atamboea. First, some kind of flat stretch of ground had to be made, for take-off, and the villagers attacked the great ant-hills with knives and swords. Then there was a further problem: Amy didn't want to waste petrol getting the engine revved up by taxying around. She wanted the tribesmen to hold the plane in position while she revved up, then let go when she gave the signal.

They eventually understood, and got hold of the struts and the tail. But as soon as Amy opened the throttle a bit, and the engine got louder, they let go of the plane and rushed away in fright. She climbed out of the cockpit and persuaded them to come back, trying hard to explain in sign language that the engine was meant to get louder, and they would come to no harm if they held the plane until she signalled. They seemed to understand – but once again, when the throttle opened, they all fled away. Not until the fourth time did they hold on long enough for Amy to get the engine up to sufficient power. The plane rushed across the clearing and took off, just clearing the trees.

It was a short but an anxious flight to Atamboea, and there proved to be just enough petrol in the tank.

Atamboea aerodrome was really just a field, with no hangars and no proper facilities. At least there was petrol, but it was in huge drums that had been standing about for so long they were covered in red rust. When the petrol was poured out, it collected rust on the way. To make sure no rust got into the engine, Amy had first to filter the petrol from the drums into smaller tins, and then filter it from those, through her chamois leathers, into the tank. There was another worry – the oil supplies that were supposed to be waiting at Atamboea had not come through. She had only one spare gallon with her, and she just had to add that to the half gallon or so of dirty oil that was left in the sump of the engine.

There was not time, now, to set off for Darwin so Amy decided to spend the rest of the day giving *Jason*'s engine a thorough overhaul. She checked every pipe and every joint for any sign of leakage, put in new plugs, and tightened up every single nut and bolt on the engine and on the plane.

It was a fine morning, cool and fresh, on Saturday, May 24th, when Amy took off, just before eight o'clock. The engine hummed along merrily, as *Jason* flew over a calm sea, and Amy kept thinking happily: 'Australia soon! Australia soon!' The dangers and disappointments of the past days now seemed like bad dreams. The flight was so smooth that time seemed to slow down – Amy would look at the clock, thinking half an hour had gone by, and discover it was only ten minutes. Then, down below, she sighted the oil tanker *Phorus*, which had been sent to the midway point of her course, just in case she was in any trouble. She swooped down and flew low over it, flinging a cake at one of the people standing on deck. The crew cheered, and Amy flew on, thinking how the ship's wireless operator would be even now sending out the signal to the world, saying she was nearing her final destination.

The next hour passed quickly, as *Jason* went smoothly on over the empty sea. Then time seemed to drag again: would Australia never show up? At last Amy saw land: Melville Island, a landmark she'd been looking out for, not far off the Australian coast. As she looked down on the surf breaking on the island's shore, she slapped *Jason*'s sides, and rocked about in her seat, cheering loudly. Then, as

The arrival in Darwin.

ON AUSTRALIAN SOIL, TAXI-ING ACROSS THE AERODROME AFTER THE LANDING

she neared the mainland, she picked up the air-cushion she had inflated, to keep her afloat if she should crash into the Timor Sea. She thumped it, yelling with delight, and then threw it over the side.

She crossed the coast and was about to look around for the aerodrome when she saw two planes ahead, waiting to escort her in. She flew between them, and saw the crowds around the airfield, gazing upwards, waiting to welcome her. Suddenly the tears came to her eyes: it was true – she had done what she set out to do, and here she was, Amy Johnson, alone in her little Gipsy Moth, *Jason*, actually landing in Australia!

7

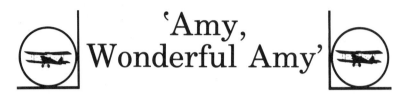

'Amy, Wonderful Amy'

It was just before four o'clock in the afternoon of May 24th, 1930, when the wheels of *Jason* first touched Australian soil, and as the little plane moved across the airfield, Amy could hardly hear the sound of its engine for the roar of the cheering crowds that had come to welcome her. She taxied to a halt, and climbed out of the cockpit, smiling. People rushed towards the plane, waving and shouting, and police had to hold them back as Amy was officially welcomed by Colonel Weddell, representing the Australian Government.

As she walked with him towards a waiting car, the crowds pressed forward, waving and cheering: an old woman hobbled up, her hand outstretched, saying 'I must touch you for luck', and burly men in wide-brimmed hats and heavy boots pushed through the crowd to shake Amy's hand. The mechanics had taken charge of *Jason*, and as the car moved away from the airfield, Amy looked back fondly at the small green plane which she thought of now as a loyal and trusted friend. Soon, they would be travelling on together, across the huge, empty continent of Australia.

Meanwhile, Amy was driven the five miles into town, along roads where there were flags at every door and window, and more people cheering and

78

waving as she passed. More cheering people packed the Town Hall for the first of many, many receptions which would fill Amy's time in the weeks to come.

In her speech replying to the Mayor of Darwin, Amy delighted her audience with her easy, natural manner, especially when she said: 'Please don't call me "Miss Johnson" – just plain "Johnnie" will do. That's what my English friends call me.' The cheers at that were greater than ever.

In spite of all she'd been through, Amy was still able to stay up late that night, as the guest of honour at a big dance. It was after eleven when she left for Colonel Weddell's house, where she was staying, and was finally able to get some sleep. She slept for eleven hours – and the next day she got up and

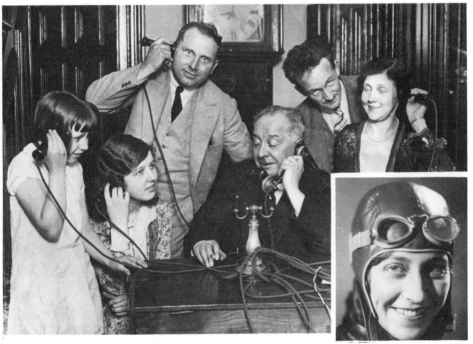

Amy's family in Hull found themselves almost as famous as she was. The picture shows (from the left) Betty, Molly, James Martin, Mr Johnson (taking the telephone call), Jack Humphreys, Mrs Johnson.

played tennis, before settling down to start replying to the hundreds and hundreds of messages of congratulation that were piling up for her. They came from the King and Queen, and VIPs of all kinds – but also from the ordinary people throughout the world who looked on Amy as a very special kind of heroine: for she too came from an 'ordinary' background, without fame or wealth or high-up connections, and it was her own grit and her own personality alone that had got her to where she was now.

And now she was headline news everywhere. The *Daily Mail* boasted about a new contract they'd arranged, by which Amy would write exclusively for them, and go on a national tour of Britain with *Jason* – and the paper even bought the plane itself. Within a few weeks of her arrival in Australia, she had recorded an account of her flight for a record company, done lots of radio broadcasts, and talked about her journey and her views on aviation for a film. The *Daily Mail* at first wanted to stop the film being shown, because of their contract with Amy; but in the end, they agreed to its release to cinemas.

Then there was also an avalanche of tributes in verse and in song:

Amy, wonderful Amy,
How can you blame me for loving you?

That's what people everywhere were singing, as the song, 'Amy', became one of the big hits of 1930. There were many other songs and dances too, with titles like 'Queen of the Air', 'The Lone Dove', and 'Aeroplane Girl'.

As for poems, Amy's flight inspired a multitude of

people to sit down and versify, in a fervour of admiration, though not necessarily in very brilliant poetry. One author wrote:

And thou hast flown the spacious world across,
Thou fair, intrepid, peerless albatross . . .

And others called Amy 'The Dancer of the Air', 'Fair Maid of Hull', 'Amazon of the Void and Space', and 'Aerial Amy! Bird of the Sky'. But perhaps the greatest sign of her fame was the fact that a playground rhyme about Amy became very popular among children; one version of it went:

She flew in an old Tin Lizzie,
Enough to make you dizzy,
And she looked so sweet
Washing her feet
In the Mediterranean Sea!

'Amy' became a popular name for new babies; biscuits were among a number of products that took Amy's name too, and one women's hockey club decided to call itself 'The Johnnie Club' from now on. There was even a new style of hat invented by a Sydney designer and called 'Jason's Quest' – it fitted the head closely like an airman's cap, and had two wings coming from over the ears and meeting in the centre of the forehead. One learned professor, writing in a Sydney newspaper, suggested that a woman pilot should now be called a 'Johnnie', instead of the clumsy word 'aviatrix' which a lot of the papers were then using.

Back in England, the press and the public were just as ecstatic about Amy as they were in Australia. She was on newsreels and radio broadcasts, and her picture was flashed on the screen at the London Coliseum, with the captions 'Queen of the Air', and 'For She's a Johnnie Good Fellow!' The Johnson family found that they were almost as famous as Amy herself. They were cheered and applauded and interviewed, and letters of congratulation arrived by the sackful. On hearing the news of Amy's safe arrival, one of the first things Mr Johnson did was to send out a radio message to the fishing fleets in the North Sea, saying that Amy had the blood of the trawling industry in her veins.

But the greatest moment of pride for the family, and for Amy, came just over a week after she got to Australia: in the King's Birthday Honours List, she was awarded the C.B.E. – Commander of the Order of the British Empire. It was an appropriate award for Amy, since she was very patriotic, and a firm believer in Britain as the Mother Country of a great Empire – in fact she was delighted when she found that the day she arrived in Darwin, 24th May, happened to be Empire Day. She regarded her great flight as helping to show how aviation could one day bring the different countries of the Empire closer together.

The day of Amy's arrival in Darwin was a Saturday, and early on the Monday morning, *Jason* was back in the air again, travelling towards Brisbane on the east coast of Australia – the capital of the state of Queensland. The distance was so great that the journey would take over three days, and to escort her over the trackless desert landscape, Amy had a special Qantas plane. She enjoyed flying over the wide plains in the bright sunshine, and often swooped down low to acknowledge the welcome of the people at the few isolated homesteads, or to get a closer look at a huge mob of sheep. Once, a group of twenty kangaroos bounded along beneath her, and she chased them for a while as they leaped and bounced across the dry earth.

Everywhere she landed, she was greeted by huge crowds – people came from remote farms and sheep stations over 100 miles away, just to get a glimpse of Amy. On the third day of the trip, the Wednesday, the escort plane guiding her went too fast, and *Jason* just wasn't able to keep up. The 'guide' became just a faint speck in the far distance, and then disappeared from sight altogether. Amy had to try to find her own way to Charleville, the place they were making for that day, with some very sketchy maps as her only navigational aid.

At least Charleville was marked as being on a railway line, so as soon as she saw that, she thought she was all right, and began to follow it. Unfortunately she was following it in the wrong direction, as she realised when it came to an end, at a little place called Quilpie. She landed there on a patch of ground dotted with tree-stumps, and had to zig-zag to avoid them. The people there were delighted at this unexpected visit, and they were able to give her directions, and supply her with motor spirit to refuel *Jason*.

At Charleville, where she was supposed to be, the crowds had waited all day to welcome her, but when the sun went down, she still hadn't arrived. So fifty cars with their headlights on were positioned around the aerodrome to guide her in, and a big flare was lit to show the wind direction. With these aids Amy was able to land safely, but the real problems came after she landed: the crowd that pushed and jostled around the plane was so thick that she found it difficult even to get out of the cockpit. In the end, four policemen wielding sticks forced their way through the mob, and a police inspector carried Amy to safety.

The following morning, Amy was able to talk by long-distance radio-telephone to her family, 11,000 miles away at 85 Park Avenue, Hull, where they all sat round a small table in the hall amidst a mass of wires, as well as reporters and photographers. Amy said she was enjoying every moment of the trip, and at the end of the call, the whole group in Hull gave three cheers down the telephone.

For them it was evening, but for Amy in Charleville it was 6.30 in the morning. When the call was over, she got ready to take *Jason* on the flight to Brisbane. It turned out to be the last time she ever piloted the plane in Australia.

During the flight, Amy found that *Jason*'s engine was spluttering and stopping when she throttled it down to run more slowly. She could cope with this all right while flying, but it became a problem when she reached Brisbane aerodrome. The escort plane went straight into land, as arranged, while Amy flew over the crowds below, at about one thousand feet.

The plan was for *Jason* to make a circuit above the airfield – a kind of Lap of Honour – before coming into land. To do this, Amy had to throttle down the engine – but when she did so, the trouble came back, the engine went dead, and the propeller stopped.

She had to act quickly, and the first essential was to lose height as fast as she could. So she tilted the plane sideways, and it slipped steeply down through the air. Nearing the ground, she levelled out to land, but by this time she was well over on the far side of the airfield, and only a few feet from the boundary fence. If she tried to turn round at that speed, she would overturn, and besides, there were other planes landing nearby. All she could do was to head straight for the fence. When she hit it, *Jason* did a somersault and stopped with a crunching crash, wings and tail badly crumpled. Amy found herself sitting upside down, still strapped into the cockpit. She wasn't hurt at all – the only damage, she discovered later, was a small tear in one of her leather boots!

She unclipped herself and slid down on to the ground. People ran forward to help her to her feet, and there was a great shout of relief from the crowds as they saw she was all right. Her first words were: 'My poor machine!'

The crash at Brisbane. This was to be the last time Amy piloted her own plane in Australia.

People swarmed around *Jason* as Amy was led away, to be greeted by the Governor of Queensland, the Premier, and the Lord Mayor of Brisbane. In spite of what she'd been through, she was able to smile and wave at the vast crowds, and make a speech of thanks. Then she was taken on a triumphal drive into the city, and she waved a red poinsettia flower, the city's emblem, at the cheering people who jammed the streets and even climbed up on to the roofs of the trams to see her.

*   *   *

The welcomes and the public appearances were beginning to exhaust Amy more than the flight from England had done. On doctor's advice, she was ordered a day's complete rest, and then fewer receptions and much less hand-shaking. And although *Jason* was being repaired, she was reluctantly persuaded, for the sake of her health, not to pilot her own plane for the rest of her Australian tour.

So, after a few days in Brisbane, she travelled as a passenger to Sydney in an Australian airliner – the first time she had ever flown in any machine larger than a two-seater. She took the controls for a short time, and said she found the plane easy enough to handle.

One of the pilots was a young Scotsman called Jim Mollison, who got chatting to Amy during the flight, and asked her if he could have a dance with her at the big Ball being held in her honour in Sydney that night. She liked the look of him, and said yes. Later he asked if he could have *two* dances, and she said

Amy flies into Sydney by airliner, while someone else pilots Jason, *above. It was on this flight that Amy first met Jim Mollison. Below, Sydney Harbour Bridge was still being built.* A contemporary Souvenir Postcard.

yes again. But at the Ball, Amy was with the Top People, including the Governor of New South Wales, and when Jim came hesitantly up to him and mentioned the dance invitations, the Governor brushed him aside. Amy didn't realise what had happened, and wondered where the charming young pilot had got to.

For the moment, anyway, she had no private life at all. In Sydney, and everywhere else on her Australian trip, there was a non-stop series of public appearances, lunches, receptions, parties, banquets and dances.

She was deluged with all kinds of gifts, including dresses and jewellery and furniture, and also umbrellas and tennis rackets, a Bible, a vacuum-cleaner, some Chinese green silk pyjamas, and an offer of free lessons in the latest dances. She had to have six secretaries to help her deal with the piles of letters and telegrams she was getting. At one reception, there was a large replica of her plane, *Jason*, made of flowers; at another, a small model of it flew all round the ballroom; at another, she was greeted by a guard of honour from a Surf Club, dressed only in bathing suits.

At every function, she had to make a speech – and luckily she found she had the knack of talking chattily and informally, with the sort of enthusiasm that immediately made her listeners warm to her.

She did have some serious things to say, about her hopes for the future of aviation, about women's role in it, and about the importance of taking every kind of safety precaution when setting out on a flight. But she could be light-hearted too – she said how much she liked dainty and delicate clothes, and was only afraid that she'd perhaps be like Cinderella, and at midnight, at a ball, the dress would change back into her old flying breeches. But she denied one newspaper report that she powdered her nose before every flight, and said: 'When I'm overhauling an engine, I don't trouble to overhaul my face as well!'

The newspapers on the whole treated Amy well, though for a while she was worried about talking to reporters because of her contract with the *Daily Mail*. But then one sensational paper, trying to boost its sales with a scandal, accused Amy of being a 'gold digger', and making a fortune out of her trip. In fact she was getting £10,000 from the *Daily Mail*, but that included writing exclusively for them, and making a strenuous tour for more than six months when she got back to Britain.

The misleading reports brought denials and sour remarks, and a deluge of hard-luck stories and begging letters, and they caused Amy a great deal of distress. Once, after she'd sent the London Aeroplane Club's chief engineer, her friend Jack Humphreys, a cable saying how all the public appearances were getting her down, he thought she wanted an excuse to come home, and sent *her* a cable saying RETURN TO ENGLAND AT ONCE. SERIOUSLY ILL. JACK. But by the time she got it, she was feeling more cheerful.

The speeches and appearances and the newspaper attacks weren't the only pressures on Amy. The two big oil and petrol companies that had helped her were battling with each other, behind the scenes, to try and get publicity out of Amy's achievement. They were both putting big advertisements in the papers, as well as trying to get her to mention them at every possible public occasion. It was really Lord Wakefield, the head of Castrol, who had done most for Amy, and she resented other firms trying to make exaggerated claims – and not just for aircraft fuel: advertisements appeared that tried to associate her flight with particular brands of cigarettes and whisky too.

Though she was often tired out, and sometimes upset, Amy rarely showed any sign of stress in public. She did once slap a man hard in the face, when he stepped forward out of a crowd, intending to kiss her – but the rest of the crowd must have felt he deserved it, for they yelled out 'Well done!' and 'Bravo, Amy!' However, most of the time, Amy managed to be as cheerful and charming as ever, and all her audiences loved her.

Crowds greet Amy outside Melbourne Town Hall.

She completely lost count of the number of speeches she had given by the time she made her last one, at the port of Fremantle, near the Western Australian capital, Perth, after six hectic weeks that had meant thousands of miles of travelling. After her stay in Sydney, she had moved on to Canberra, Melbourne, Adelaide, and then Perth, with lots of visits in between. In her farewell speech, she thanked the Australian people for all their kindness, and repeated her faith in the future of flying as a regular means of travel, saying she was convinced there would one day be regular airline flights between England and Australia.

She talked about women pilots too, and said they ought to learn all about the technical side of their aeroplanes, and not expect to do what some of them did, putting on smart flying-suits and sauntering to the aerodrome, where their machines waited for them, all ready and prepared by experts. She said it was time now to get on with her job, which was flying: she wasn't built for a constant round of social engagements and festivities – aviation was what she considered her 'life's work'.

In pouring rain, Amy Johnson climbed the gangway stairs on to her ship, and gave a final wave to the huge crowd that had gathered to give their heroine a good send-off. Then she went to her cabin, which was specially decorated in her honour, and thought how good it would be to relax for a while on this ocean liner, recovering her strength to face the crowded schedule of her British tour, and before that, the tumultuous welcome that awaited the 'Queen of the Air' when she arrived at Croydon Aerodrome . . .

8

 A Life
of Glamour

In the weeks before she left England on her great
flight, Amy sometimes imagined how nice it would
be to come back home quietly and surprise her
friends at the London Aeroplane Club. She would
land unnoticed in a corner of the airfield, during the
lunch-hour, then creep into the hangar and put on
her old overalls; and when her friends came back
from lunch, she'd just say 'Well, I said I'd do it, and I
did!' – and then get down to work, giving *Jason* a
really good clean.

That certainly wasn't the way it worked out in
reality. She got off the liner at Port Said in Egypt,
and flew as a passenger on the regular air service,
first to Vienna, and then on to Croydon, the aerodrome where her journey had begun just three
months earlier. Her plane, *Jason*, had been brought
home by ship, and was there on the tarmac among
the waiting crowds.

Amy arrived as it was beginning to get dark, on
August Bank Holiday Monday, to a welcome from
her family, Government Ministers, and crowds
totalling more than a million people; they thronged
the aerodrome, and lined the streets of London for
the whole 12-mile drive to Grosvenor House in
Mayfair, the hotel where the Johnson family were
staying.

92

Though she was cold and tired Amy went out on to the balcony and stood, holding a huge bouquet of flowers, and smiling and waving to the upturned faces of the crowds below. Then there were more speeches and congratulations, and questions fired at her by the jostling newspapermen, and it was after two o'clock in the morning by the time Amy got to bed.

The rest of that week was packed with activity – as well as official receptions and speeches and interviews, Amy managed to do some flying, go shopping with her mother, and make a family visit to a theatre, where they were nearly mobbed by the delighted crowds. There was a mountain of fan-mail and invitations to be dealt with, too.

The next morning, Amy flew up to Hull in *Jason*, and the welcome there, in her home-town, was even more loud and joyful than it had been in London. There were receptions and processions and dinners, and a huge rally for young people at the City Hall, which moved Amy so much that she said she'd decided to present a special Cup to be awarded every year to a boy or girl from Hull, for some act of courage. And the Amy Johnson Cup For Courage is still presented.

Back in London, she attended a big ceremony in Hyde Park where she was given a new aeroplane, bought with money subscribed by the readers of a daily newspaper. The De Havilland aircraft company, which made her original plane, had also presented her with a new one, so she now had a *Jason Two* and a *Jason Three*, the first *Jason* having been bought by the *Daily Mail* as part of their deal with Amy.

*August Bank Holiday, 1930. More than a million people gathered at Croydon
Airport and on the road to London to welcome home Amy Johnson.* Jason *had
been brought back from Australia and was already on the tarmac.*

After a short holiday in Wales with her sister
Molly, Amy set off to fulfil the rest of that deal – the
national tour which had been arranged. By this
time, though, Amy's health was starting to suffer
from the strain of being a celebrity – the rushing
about, the endless smiling and speech-making and
shaking hands. She was pleased and touched that so
many people wanted to see her and wish her well,
but she was beginning to feel as though she was
acting a part, and that her real self was being lost in
the cheers and applause for 'Amy Johnson, Queen of
the Air'.

After visiting only a few of the places on the tour
programme, Amy decided she would have to abandon
the rest of it, or collapse completely. So she flew *Jason*
back to her own base, the London Aeroplane Club,

The triumphal drive through London.

Amy and her family all stayed at the Grosvenor House hotel in London.

and persuaded the *Daily Mail* to let her off the remainder of the tour.

She spent the next couple of months partly in a nursing home and partly staying with friends, and when she was fit again she moved into a flat in north London, not too far from the Aeroplane Club. But she still felt restless and lonely, and she still felt the pressure of fame: every day she was getting at least twenty invitations to make public appearances, and the post brought many times that number of fan letters. She was now so much of a celebrity that no one could think of offering her some ordinary, regular job in aviation – yet proving she could do such a job was one of the main reasons she had flown to Australia.

She decided that the only thing to do was to make another long-distance flight, and this time she chose China as her destination. She set off to fly east across Europe on New Year's day, 1931, ignoring the warnings of experts who said it was suicide to try and fly a small plane across the freezing wastes of Siberia in the middle of winter.

It was lucky, perhaps, that she never got as far as Siberia, but had to make a forced landing in fog, in a forest clearing in Poland. She travelled on to Moscow by train, where she was pleased at the praise and the welcome she got from top aviation officials. Though her crashed plane, *Jason Three*, had been repaired in Poland, she decided against going on with her flight just then – instead, she would have another go when the weather was better.

This time, she took her engineer friend and former teacher, Jack Humphreys, as co-pilot and mechanic, and they travelled in the plane De Havilland's had given her, *Jason Two*. They set off at the end of July, with Japan as their destination, and crossing the vast plains and forests of Siberia they found their way by following the course of the Trans-Siberian Railway far below them.

They reached Tokyo in ten days, breaking the record, and they got a great reception from the crowds and from the officials, who were led by General Nagaoka, President of the Japanese Imperial Aviation Society. He had already sent Amy a photograph of himself, which was probably just as well, as otherwise she might have got something of a shock: the General had a white moustache which stuck out ten inches on each side of his face, like long wispy flags – and when he welcomed Amy with a kiss on both cheeks, the moustache tickled her neck!

In Japan, there were more receptions and speeches – Amy attended a banquet dressed in a kimono, and waving an oriental fan, and was cheered by throngs of Japanese men waving their hard straw hats –

Amy's second great long-distance flight, with Jack Humphreys in Jason Two, *was to Japan. In Tokyo, she danced with General Nagaoka.*

hats very like the one that Amy so disliked when she had to wear it at school.

By coincidence, Jack and Amy arrived in Japan just as another record-breaking pilot arrived in London: it was Jim Mollison, who had just completed the solo journey from Australia in only nine days. Amy sent him a cable of congratulation, saying she hoped they would meet when she got back to England, and he replied saying he'd look forward to that. But they didn't in fact meet until over eight months later, and then it was far away from both London and Tokyo – in Cape Town, in South Africa.

When she got back to England from Japan, Amy started on a lecture tour, using slides to illustrate a talk about her flight to Australia. The tour was very popular, but had to be cut short when she became very ill and had an operation. To convalesce, she chose a form of travel she always liked – a sea voyage on an ocean liner, the *Winchester Castle*, bound for South Africa. It arrived in Cape Town on the day Jim Mollison was due there, at the end of a solo long-distance flight from England.

Amy went to the airport, and this time, instead of being the flyer everyone was waiting for, she was one of the waiting crowd, peering into the sky and listening for the distant throb of an engine. But Jim didn't appear out of the sky at all – he arrived at the airport in a taxi, having landed his plane on a beach! She pressed her way through the crowd, and finally managed to welcome him and to have a brief chat, in an aerodrome office with dozens of curious faces peering in through the windows. She went into the town with him, and helped him deal with the mass of cables and congratulatory messages that were waiting for him at his hotel. The next day they had lunch together, and then Amy continued her trip on the *Winchester Castle*, first to Durban and then back to England.

Soon after she got back, she met Jim again – he was at the aerodrome when she returned from a flight to an Air Display in Antwerp. He asked her to have lunch with him the following day. They met at Quaglino's, an expensive and fashionable restaurant, which Jim nonchalantly called 'a discreet feeding-house in the West End'. They talked about aviation, and about the flights they had made and those they hoped to make in the future.

The conversation was lively, and Amy smiled happily, delighted to be in the company of this attractive and adventurous young man. Jim was delighted with *her*, too – so much so, that near the end of the meal he suddenly leaned across the table and asked Amy to marry him. She didn't hesitate, but accepted at once – and so began a partnership that was to bring Amy more fame and more adventure, but a great deal of sorrow, too.

For the moment, though, she was wildly happy, as Jim whirled her into the hectic social life he enjoyed so much: a life of cocktail parties, heavy drinking, fast cars, lavish meals, night-clubs, and big spending. Jim liked to be seen as a playboy, a man-about-town who lived life dangerously and lived it to the full. An engagement between two such celebrities delighted the gossip columnists and the public, and the pair's activities were the subject of daily reports and photographs in the papers.

Jim loved to be in the spotlight like that, but Amy

was less enthusiastic. She enjoyed going to the south of France, meeting film stars, buying fur coats and new dresses – many of them black, which was Jim's favourite colour – but she found the continual parties and late nights tiring, and she worried about the amount of drink Jim managed to pour down his throat, and about the way he spent money as if there was going to be no tomorrow.

They went to Scotland to meet Jim's mother and family – his parents had been divorced when he was ten – and they went to meet Amy's family in Bridlington, the seaside resort not far from Hull, where the Johnsons had moved the year before. Amy's parents had been startled by the suddenness of her engagement, and were doubtful about the fast life she now lived, but friends like Jack Humphreys told them not to worry: the couple seemed very much in love, and totally delighted with each other.

Jim was planning a two-way transatlantic solo flight that summer, and no date had been set for the wedding, though the papers were always full of rumours. Amy told her parents not to take any notice of these, so they were surprised and hurt one evening to discover that the rumours were correct. The papers said Amy and Jim were to marry the following day – and after phone-calls and telegrams between Bridlington and London, the Johnsons learned from Amy that indeed she was going to get married next day. She said they wanted to keep it a completely private ceremony with no publicity.

The Johnsons were bewildered and sad at the sudden, casual way Amy had let them know about the wedding, and they wondered what to do. It was already late at night when Mr Johnson said: 'Well –

Amy married Jim Mollison wearing his favourite colour – black! They planned the wedding so suddenly that even Amy's family did not attend.

if you'd all really like to go to the wedding, then we'll go!'

It was nearly three o'clock in the morning, and raining hard, when Amy's parents finally set off in their car to drive more than 200 miles through the night. With them were Amy's sisters Molly and Betty, and Molly's fiancé, Trevor. They drove without stopping, hoping desperately that they would be in time. But when they got to London and the church in Hanover Square, at half past ten, the ceremony had finished. A Rolls-Royce drove Amy and Jim Mollison away through the cheering, gaping crowds that had gathered, to a champagne celebration with a few friends.

The Johnsons were too timid to follow, so they had a gloomy breakfast and climbed back into their car for the return journey, depressed and very hurt. Amy was very upset later on, when she learned what had happened, but even if her behaviour was mainly due to confusion, and Jim Mollison's tactless, rushed way of doing things, it was a long time before her family could altogether forgive her.

Jim was due to make his transatlantic flight in a couple of weeks, starting from Ireland, so there was only time for a short honeymoon. They spent it staying with a friend at a castle in Scotland, and they flew north, each piloting a new plane, and racing each other to arrive first. Amy won by five minutes. Jim told reporters at the airport that he wouldn't be surprised if she suddenly decided to race him all the way across the Atlantic too!

But when the time came, Amy went with him to Dublin, where his plane *Hearts Content* took off from a mile-long stretch of beach; then she came back to London to wait for news. Since there was no radio contact with planes in flight, Amy could only know that Jim had got safely across the Atlantic when he was sighted on the other side. Eventually,'the news came: Jim Mollison had landed in Newfoundland, after making the first-ever solo flight over the Atlantic from east to west, in the record time of 31 hours and 20 minutes.

Three months later, Amy too set off to break a solo flying record – the one from England to Cape Town in South Africa, set up the previous year, by . . . Jim Mollison!

9
The Flying Mollisons

When Jim came back from the USA, he and Amy were able to spend some time at home together – 'home' being a luxury apartment in Grosvenor House. They lived a busy social life, and were always in demand for public appearances at Air Displays and Air Pageants, and ceremonies to name new aircraft.

But in spite of her glamourous life, Amy still took flying very seriously, and when she was preparing for her attempt on Jim's Cape Town record, she got herself really fit by going skating every evening, and giving up smoking and alcoholic drinks. She also took some lessons in 'flying blind', using only instruments, because this trip would mean doing some of her flying by night.

Jim helped her to plan the journey, and lent her the extra petrol tanks from his plane, and the maps he had used on his own flight to South Africa. And he was all ready to fly off in search of Amy if she got lost: Amy said she realised *that* was a story the newspapers would really love!

They never got the chance to write it, though Amy did have some nasty moments during her journey: she found the blind-flying instruments hard to cope with, especially when the plane was bumping about in the middle of a rainstorm on a dark night, and she knew there were mountains somewhere down there below. But she kept to the route she had planned, and flew south along the west coast of Africa, encouraged by cables from Jim.

She completed the trip in four and a half days, beating his record by ten hours. There was a big welcome at the airport, and soon after she arrived she was able to get Jim's excited congratulations in a long-distance phone call from London. Then she was thankful to sink into a feather-bed and sleep for 14 hours. She had only managed to get a total of about five hours' sleep during the whole journey.

When she woke, she was delighted to find that among the messages congratulating her, there was one from King George the Fifth himself.

Amy spent nearly a month in South Africa, waiting for the full moon which would help her find her way on the flight back. It was summer there, and she enjoyed the sunbathing, tennis and swimming, but she was glad when the time came to climb once more into her plane, *Desert Cloud*.

The name was all too apt: the 'clouds' she flew into in the desert were tall, whirling spirals of choking sand, whipped up by the wind. There were ordinary clouds in other places, as well as heavy rain and dense fog, and she lost her way several times. Once, her plane was being so bumped about by high winds that she decided to land – but even on the ground the gale nearly blew the aircraft away as she clung to it.

The weather got calmer once she reached Europe, and she landed at Croydon Aerodrome just a week before Christmas, to a tremendous welcome from the crowds.

There were headlines in all the newspapers, as

Jim Mollison sees Amy off in Desert Cloud *on her flight to South Africa to beat his own record.*

well as commercial advertisements for the brand of petrol she had used, and for the type of oil – described rather wordily as an 'absolutely reliable and peerless lubricant'. One popular Sunday paper was starting to serialise her life story.

Amy was even more pleased to find that her achievement was being praised too by the serious aviation magazines, which sometimes sneered at flyers who made headline-catching journeys. One of these magazines once said that flying the Atlantic was dead easy: you just had to point the plane's nose towards the west, go on until you saw land, and then turn left! But there were no such sneers now for Amy, only praise: and her proudest moment came when she was given the 1932 Segrave Trophy, one of the big awards in the world of flying.

She and Jim spent Christmas in the fashionable winter-sports resort of St Moritz, among a glittering Smart Set that included famous film stars and producers. Amy loved it all, spending energetic days skiing, skating or bob-sleighing, and the evenings at dances and parties where she was able to show off her beautiful dresses, like the one given her on her way through Paris by the famous dress designer, Coco Chanel.

In the New Year, life didn't get any calmer for the Flying Mollisons. In February, Jim was off again on another solo flight across the Atlantic, this time to South America. He was the first person to make the east-west flight there, and the first solo flyer to have crossed both the North and the South Atlantic Ocean. He was back in the limelight again – in fact, he and Amy seemed to be taking it in turns!

But it was now getting harder to find new 'Firsts' and new spectacular flights to do, and harder to get publicity for them, as the public began to get used to the daring deeds of pilots. Yet publicity was something the pilots had to have, in order to get financial backing, commercial tie-ups and newspaper deals – that, together with any prize money they got, was how they earned their living.

Amy knew the value of publicity, though her attitude to it was very different from Jim's: he revelled in the fame and the glamour, but she was much more shy, in spite of her easy and natural charm – she often wished she could just be one of the crowd again, and step out of the spotlight, but there seemed no chance of doing that.

They planned to make their next flight together, and to make it a sensational one: an attempt on the world long-distance record. Their plane was a new twin-engined aircraft, which they painted Jim's favourite colour, black, and named *Seafarer*. It was designed to carry passengers, but they took out the passenger-seats and put in extra petrol tanks instead. Their plan was to fly to New York, and then start the record-breaking attempt from there, flying all the way back over the Atlantic, carrying on eastwards across Europe and the Mediterranean, and finally landing in the Middle East, at Baghdad.

Amy's parents and Jim's mother were at Croydon to give them a send-off. Amy always liked to have mascots and good-luck charms with her, and this time she had a number of medallions of St Christopher, the patron saint of travellers. *Seafarer* was weighed down with over 400 gallons of fuel, and needed an extra long run for take-off; so Jim taxied out past the runway and on to the grass verge at the edge of the airfield. Starting its run, the plane hit a dip in the ground, swung round and sank to the grass with its undercarriage broken.

The Mollisons were angry and embarrassed at their failure, but the crash certainly made headline news. They must have thought that St Christopher hadn't been much help – but Amy's father tried to comfort her by saying that if they hadn't had the medallions on board, perhaps something worse might have happened.

Amy and Jim were determined to try again, and to give themselves a long enough take-off run they decided to leave from a beach on the Welsh coast called Pendine Sands. While they waited for the right weather over the Atlantic, it was hard to get away from sightseers – but they sometimes managed it: one woman remembered driving past a small lake in the hills and seeing a homely-looking couple there, the husband fishing and the wife sitting nearby, knitting. It was the Mollisons – and for once, there wasn't a photographer in sight.

But there were plenty of them when they eventually took off, at noon on July 22nd, with *Seafarer* needing a take-off run of about a mile along the sands. They soon ran into clouds and fog, and flew over them at 2,000 feet. They had bad weather until they were over 800 miles out over the sea. Because they were flying west towards the sun, the twilight lasted till midnight by their time. Then they spent a good night flying above clouds.

Amy admired Jim's skill at navigating, as they ran into fog again during the next day. When it cleared they could see icebergs and chunks of ice drifting on the water.

Almost exactly 24 hours after they had set off, they sighted land: it was the coast of Newfoundland. They turned south, but there was still a long way to go to New York, and as the day went on they began to wonder if their supplies of petrol would last out. Amy wanted to stop at Boston to refuel, but Jim said they must press on. It was getting dark, and they still had 50 miles to go, when they realised their fuel was nearly exhausted.

They were near an aerodrome at Bridgeport, and Jim circled it and then came into land. *Seafarer* was still moving quite fast when they saw the boundary fence looming up ahead of them. The plane overshot the end of the runway and ran into marshy land beyond the boundary and turned over, with a crash and a crunch of wings and fuselage. They were flung

New 'firsts' in flying were becoming harder to find. The Mollisons planned a spectacular joint attempt on the world long-distance record. They set out in Seafarer from the Pendine Sands in south Wales, where the heavily-laden plane could have a mile-long take-off run.

Seafarer off the coast of Ireland, bound for New York.

out of the plane and Jim was knocked unconcious, his head cut and bleeding, while Amy had bad cuts and bruises on her arms and legs.

They were taken to hospital where their injuries were treated and bandaged, and Jim had thirty stitches in his face. Meanwhile, souvenir hunters descended on the mangled remains of *Seafarer* like vultures and stripped it bare.

*   *   *

Though their world-record attempt had been a failure, the Mollisons' dramatic crash made them big news, and Amy soon became the smiling heroine of the papers and the newsreels in America, just as she had been in Australia. They were driven through New York City, which gave them its

The Mollisons, injured when Seafarer *crashed at Bridgeport, were invited to lunch with President Roosevelt.*

New York gives the Mollisons its traditional 'ticker-tape welcome'.

traditional 'ticker-tape welcome', with office workers
in the skyscrapers flinging down the long white
streamers of paper from the telex news machines.

They were invited to lunch by the President
himself, Franklin D. Roosevelt, together with
Amelia Earhart and her husband. Amelia, the first
woman to fly the Atlantic, was a serious and
practical pilot like Amy, with a great belief in the
future of aviation – and the two became firm friends.

Amy was very impressed with the way the air-

111

lines were organised in the United States, both for passengers and for airmail. She stayed on in America, studying the flying situation as well as aircraft design and manufacture, and enjoying the company of Amelia and other flying enthusiasts. Jim went to and fro, across the Atlantic, getting a replacement for *Seafarer* and preparing for their long-distance record attempt. They planned to take off from the shore of one of the Canadian Great Lakes, but the heavily loaded plane just wouldn't get off the ground, and they finally decided to give up the whole idea.

Though Amy was much happier in America than she had been with the hectic cocktail-party life-style she had had in London, she wanted to get back there to Jim, who was now busy arranging a new venture – they were going to compete in an Air Race from England to Australia, with a prize of £15,000.

Their plane was one of a new kind of racing-plane called the Comet, and they named it *Black Magic*. The first part of the race went so well for them that they got to Karachi in 22 hours, which was half the previous record time. But after that they were in trouble: one engine packed up altogether just before they reached Allahabad, and they had to land there and wait for it to be repaired, with no chance now of completing the race.

It began to look as if the Flying Mollisons had passed the peak of their fame and success, though Amy was pleased at the professional recognition she was getting: in 1934 she was elected President of the Women's Engineering Society, and that was the kind of honour she valued much more than being a glamorous figure in the press.

The papers, however, had been carrying gossip as well as glamour – there were rumours that Amy and Jim's marriage was not going smoothly. The stories worried Amy's parents, who were comforted to read a strong denial by Jim that anything was wrong. But there was fact behind the rumours: Amy hated Jim's heavy drinking, and began to suspect his relationships with other women. Their dashing-around lives meant frequent absences from each other, and in 1935, the year after the Air Race failure, the absences got longer, with Jim going off to America and Amy to Madeira, for a long rest and holiday to restore her failing health.

She was still very much in love with Jim, even though they were drifting apart, and she wrote to her father saying that she knew Jim had made her life unhappy, yet she would do just the same if she had the chance over again. She was unhappy with him, but unhappy away from him, too. And she said, forlornly: 'All women are fools enough to love the men who hurt them most'.

Back in London, they were together again for a while, and even started to plan a regular Atlantic air-cargo service. The idea petered out, and by the end of the year their marriage had almost done the same. They agreed to live apart, for some time at least.

Amy spent a lot of time in Paris, and made plans with a French backer to start a firm organising pleasure cruises by air. But she abandoned these temporarily, in order to prepare for another solo record-breaking flight . . .

10
Last Flight

Amy's destination was once again to be Cape Town, and she was trying to get the record back from Flight-Lieutenant Tommy Rose, who had recently flown there from England in just under four days.

Her aircraft was a monoplane called a Percival Gull, and it had an enclosed cabin, so she was able to set off wearing a smart blue suit instead of the flying kit and goggles needed for an open cockpit. The plane had special long-range tanks which could carry enough fuel for the most difficult part of the journey – 2,000 miles across the Sahara Desert. But when she was making her take-off run on the stony airfield of the French Foreign Legion post of Colomb Béchar in North Africa, the heavily loaded plane suddenly swung round, and the undercarriage collapsed.

The plane needed spare parts for repairs, and eventually Amy decided to get an airline plane back home, and bring them out herself. She flew back to Colomb Béchar with a mechanic, a pilot friend, Peter Reiss, and her sister Molly, who had asked if she could come along on the trip as an extra 'spare part'. When they came in to land, they were surprised when a line of horsemen thundered towards and past them, in a special kind of spectacular charge performed for honoured visitors. It turned out that they had been expecting the Head of the Foreign Legion! But when they discovered it was Amy, they did the charge again, in *her* honour.

The Legionnaires entertained them well for several days while the plane was repaired. They visited some of the nearby oases in the desert, which Amy thought were very beautiful – she even had the idea of including them in the aeroplane pleasure-cruises she hoped to arrange.

When the plane was repaired, they returned to London, and a couple of days before she was due to set out again for Cape Town, Jim turned up, saying he hoped they could get together once more. Amy agreed, and he moved into her small London house. He was at the airfield at Gravesend to see her off, on a Monday morning in May.

Amy had decided not to leave the day before, because she'd become superstitious about setting off

At Colomb Béchar, the Foreign Legion gave Amy a ceremonial charge-past.

on a Sunday – she said that it was a strange coincidence that every accident she'd had had happened on a Sunday, so she wasn't taking any
chances.

Nothing on the first stages of the journey seemed
to be how she had pictured it. Instead of the calm
blue of the Mediterranean, she ran into dusty,
swirling mists blown up by the hot wind that comes
at that season, and had to climb to 11,000 feet to
get above them. Then, after a refuelling stop at
Oran, she waited for a weather report, and set off
over the Sahara Desert. She had imagined herself
flying in a clear sky with a large white moon, gazing
down on endless stretches of sand, like a huge,
moonlit beach.

Instead, her wait for the weather report had made
her late, and the moon soon set; she found herself
flying blind most of the way, relying on her instruments. She nearly lost her way in heavy mists,
but at last when it got light she was able to find the
River Niger and follow its course to a place called
Niamey.

The airfield surface there was soft and swampy,
and she didn't dare to take off with a full load, so she
had to make a shorter hop than she had meant to,
landing thankfully on the coast at Cotonou on a
newly-made runway. From there she made another
night flight, through storm-clouds and lightning
flashes, landing at dawn on a marshy airfield where
the wheels of the plane sank into the bog. She took
off again only by keeping the engine at full blast,
with people pushing on both wings, and then she
found the airfield grass so long that it was like
taking off through a forest. The plane just got off the

ground before reaching the boundary. After nearly getting stuck again at the next airfield, this time in soft sand, Amy took off after dark, flying between two huge fires lit at the edge of the field to show her the right direction. She finally completed the 6,700 mile journey to Cape Town in 3 days, 6 hours and 26 minutes, beating the previous record by more than 11 hours.

Three days later, she took off on the return flight, and set up a record for that, too, as well as for the round trip. The chorus of praise that greeted her was as loud as it had ever been: an English and a French

One of the many advertisements which appeared after Amy's Cape Town flight.

By 1939 aeroplane design had changed, so that Amy Mollison was able to pilot her Percival Gull to Cape Town in an enclosed cabin, wearing this smart Schiaparelli suit instead of the flying kit and goggles needed in an open cockpit.

newspaper paid large sums for her exclusive story, and her name was used in advertisements not only for oil and petrol, but for the plane's brakes, wireless, and lubrication system, too.

Amy was given new titles like 'Queen of the Four Winds', and one of the many poetic tributes called her 'the girl who sweeps the cobwebs from the corners of the skies'!

There was another avalanche of fan letters too. By this time Amy and Jim were really experts when it came to examining the style and content of fan letters: in fact, Jim once did a rough count of the different kinds of letters they got. He reckoned that about half were pure congratulations, a quarter were from inventors, would-be pilots, or people asking for information, and the rest were begging or abusive, with a few from religious fanatics who thought flying was sinful, and said that if God had meant men to fly, he would have given them wings.

The same, presumably, applied to women, so the religious objectors would have little comfort in the year 1936: besides Amy's Cape Town records, there were other historic flights by pilots like Jean Batten, who flew the 14,000 miles from England to New Zealand in just over 11 days, and Beryl Markham, who crossed the Atlantic in 24 hours, making the first east-west solo transatlantic flight by a woman. It was also the year when Britain's first air hostess was appointed – on the regular service between London and Paris.

But sadly, it was not a good year for Amy's marriage: she finally couldn't tolerate Jim's affairs with other women any more, and started divorce proceedings against him. Early in 1937 she changed her name back to 'Amy Johnson' by official Deed Poll.

Her flying career was to have its disappointments, too: her scheme for the air pleasure cruises came to nothing, partly because her wealthy French colleague wanted to have a romantic as well as a business relationship with her, but she found she felt nothing for him except intense irritation!

Then she went to the United States and took advanced lessons in navigation. She hoped to take part in a big transatlantic Air Race from New York to Paris, but the race was cancelled.

Not long afterwards, Amy's friend, Amelia Earhart, was lost over the Pacific Ocean, making a long-distance flight.

Though she was still a famous name, Amy began to shun the city and the glamorous life she had been leading: she moved to country places, first to the Chiltern Hills and then the Cotswolds. She did a lot of writing for newspapers and magazines, not only about aviation, but also about cars and driving, and about gliding, which was a sport she got very enthusiastic over: in fact she once said that sailing smoothly and gently through the sky in a glider was the next best thing to graduating as an angel! She forecast that flying on airlines would soon become such an everyday thing that people would turn to gliding for real enjoyment. It was indeed less than ten years since Amy's epic flight to Australia, and then she was one of the few people who believed that air travel would one day become a regular method of transport. Now, air routes had grown so much that Amy was able to write a whole book about their development, called *Sky Roads of the World*.

She still did some flying, and she was still anxious for some kind of regular job in the aviation world, but all she was offered was a junior post in the Air Ministry. At last, in the summer of 1939, she did get a job as a professional pilot, for an air ferry firm operating on the south coast of England and the Isle of Wight. A few months later, in September, the Second World War began. The firm was taken over by the Government and she was kept on to do military ferrying work, together with the other pilots. Then, in May 1940, she joined the women's section of the Air Transport Auxiliary – the ATA – whose main job was to pilot aircraft between the various RAF bases, as well as from the factories to the airfields.

She was based at Hatfield, north of London, and she really enjoyed the work, though it involved long hours and often a great deal of hanging about, waiting for the weather to clear. But now she was doing what she'd always wanted to do – a regular flying job as a professional pilot. And she was happy to be just one of the group, with no special position or privileges – even though she was recognised at every airfield she went to, and surrounded by a throng of servicemen asking for autographs. She wore the same uniform as her colleagues – blue slacks and tunic, and a little cap that perched on the head – and followed the same routine.

An ATA pilot never knew exactly what job she'd be given each day, until she reported to the Duty Pilot, and was told what kind of aircraft she had to fly, and where from and where to.

Besides checking on the weather situation, she had to make other preparations too, like finding out

After the break-up of her marriage, Amy began to avoid big-city life and moved to the country. Gliding was one of her favourite sports.

where the big defensive barrage balloons would be floating in the sky, and what the day's special 'Signals' were – these were like a password you had to give if you were challenged by a ground control station or another aircraft. Then the pilot was taken by one of the planes that acted as 'taxis', to the aerodrome where her own plane was. She flew it to its destination, and then had to make her way back to base – if she was lucky, there'd be a 'taxi' plane going, but otherwise she had to go by train or bus, or even to hitch-hike.

Sometimes bad weather meant that pilots could be stuck at some distant aerodrome for days, and that was why Amy spent Christmas 1940 at Prestwick in Scotland, unable to join her parents in Bridlington, or to get to Blackpool, which was now the home of Amy's sister Molly and her husband, Trevor.

Amy was back in Scotland soon after the New

Year began, to take a plane south to Kidlington in Oxfordshire. The weather got bad on the way, but she was able to get as far as the airfield near Blackpool, so she went to stay the night with Molly and Trevor. Amy talked to her parents on the telephone, and wished them a Happy New Year. She and Molly and Trevor had a cheerful evening, and Molly gave Amy her Christmas presents – some satin underclothes, and an oval mirror with little flowers carved on the frame. Amy wrapped the gifts again in their Christmas paper, and packed them in her hold-all bag.

She talked about her life in the ATA, and seemed contented and proud to be working to help the RAF and the war effort.

Now she was landing almost daily at RAF airfields, but Molly remembered the time she had flown with Amy, and landed at one where they were not expected. It was before the War, some years ago, when Amy was taking her old plane, the first *Jason*, on its last flight from Hull down to London. (It was to have an honoured placed on permanent display at the Science Museum, where it can still be seen.) Molly went along for the trip, remarking before they started that there only seemed to be one parachute. Amy said that if they got into any trouble, and had to bale out, Molly could hold on to her, and they'd go down together. Luckily it didn't come to that, though they did have some trouble with *Jason*'s engine, and made an emergency landing at an airfield they saw below them. A man in uniform rushed up to the plane, shouting: 'You can't land here – this is RAF!' Then he recognised Amy, and asked if he could have her autograph.

Throughout her flying career, Amy never had to use her parachute – until that day in 1941, when she flew off from Blackpool on her way to Kidlington.

It was a Sunday – but Amy had a job to do, and she couldn't afford to be superstitious now. At breakfast in the morning, Molly looked out of the window at the mist and the clouds, and said: 'Amy – you can't possibly fly today'.

But Amy said, 'It's an RAF plane, and the boys are waiting for it. I've got to go. Don't worry – I'll fly over the top of the clouds, and smell my way to Kidlington!'

Outside the house, Amy turned and smiled at Molly and her young daughter, standing waving at the window. It was the last they ever saw of her.

She took off from the airfield near Blackpool just before noon. At half past three that afternoon, sailors on a Navy ship in the Thames Estuary saw a parachutist come down out of the clouds, and soon afterwards an aeroplane crashed into the sea.

The captain of the ship, Lieutenant-Commander Fletcher, altered course and steamed full speed ahead in that direction. Soon they saw someone in the rough, heaving water of the sea, drifting towards the ship. It was a girl in a flying-helmet. She came to within three yards of the stern of the ship, and one of the sailors threw a rope out towards her. She made no attempt to grab hold of it, but simply called out: 'Hurry, please hurry!' Then the stern of the ship was lifted up by a huge wave, and crashed down again, on top of her. She was never seen again.

But peering out into the driving sleet and snow and the grey swell of the sea, the people on the ship thought they could see another person floating

there. Lieutenant-Commander Fletcher dived over-
board and swam through the freezing water. For a
while he seemed to be floating, holding up what
could have been the head of someone in a flying-
helmet. Then he let go of it. A lifeboat was lowered
from the ship, and the crew pulled Commander
Fletcher from the water. He was unconscious, and
died soon afterwards.

With him died the true answer to a mystery that
was a sensation in the papers at the time, and was
never fully solved, in spite of the most careful in-
vestigations. There was no doubt that it was Amy
who died under the stern of the ship, and no doubt
that it was her plane that crashed: her two bags
were picked up from the sea – in fact there wasn't
even a crack in the oval mirror that Molly had given
her.

The mystery is: was Amy carrying a passenger,
and if so, who was it? Those who think she did have
someone else with her have various theories.
Perhaps she stopped to give a friend a lift – but it
was strictly against ATA rules to take anyone as a
passenger without permission, and Amy was a
conscientious pilot, unlikely to flout the rules.
Perhaps she was on a secret mission, and had flown
over to France to drop or pick up a British agent
there – but no evidence or record has been found to
support this theory. She certainly didn't take anyone with her when she left the airfield near Blackpool – there were many witnesses who said she was
quite alone.

The most probable answer is that she never had
anyone with her at all – she simply lost her way in
the fog and cloud and snow going to Kidlington,

the wings got covered in ice, and she was forced down, baling out as the plane descended. The bags that were recovered were made of leather – one of them could easily have been mistaken for a flying helmet, as it floated in the water. It was some distance from the ship, the sea was rough, and visibility was very bad. Perhaps Commander Fletcher swam to it, realised his mistake, floated for a short time, holding on to the bag, then let go. No one will ever know for certain.

In St Paul's Cathedral there is a memorial to the 173 men and women of the ATA, from many nations, who gave their lives during the Second World War. Amy would surely have been proud to be among that number. She is remembered in all sorts of other ways: in street names, an aviation scholarship, the Cup she presented for the young people of Hull, the Museum at Sewerby Hall, Bridlington, which contains her trophies and awards and all sorts of other personal relics.

But she lives most lastingly as the young, delightful girl whose courage and dedication to flying made her a world-wide legend: Amy Johnson – Queen of the Air.

Acknowledgements and Thanks

I should like to give special thanks to Mrs Molly Jones, Amy Johnson's sister, for her help and encouragement with this book. She also kindly supplied a number of the photographs, from her personal albums.

I am also grateful to the Women's Engineering Society, the Royal Air Force Museum Archives, the British Library, the Radio Times Hulton Picture Library, the British Women Pilots' Association, the Royal Aeronautical Society, British Aerospace, the Amy Johnson Collection at Sewerby Hall, Bridlington, and the Information Department of the City of Kingston-upon-Hull.

Amy Johnson's own book about the world's air routes is called *Sky Roads of the World*, and she also contributed an essay about her younger days to a book called *Myself When Young*. The fullest account of her life is in the authorised biography, *Amy Johnson*, by Constance Babington Smith.

Gordon Snell

Index

127

Index

128